They Call Me Farang

Dedicated to my mother and to my wife Beau.

Table of Contents

Adventures Wait 1

Lady Thai...6

Jerseys...28

Ninety Grand 40

The Texan 56

The Art of Nose Picking 63

Noise Pollution 68

The Faucet 78

When You Gotta Go, Go! 84

Thai Bar Girls 91

One Last Fight 96

Thai Woman vs. American Women 104

Settling Down...109

Growing Old 113

Observations On Aging 123

Paradise...128

Shades of Green...134

Looking Ahead 139

Ten Things Learned from Living in Thailand 145

Cheat Sheet...151

Adventures Wait

"The purpose of life is to live it, to taste experience to the utmost, to reach out eagerly and without fear for newer and richer experiences."

Eleanor Roosevelt,
American Politician and the First Lady of the United States

***

In the 1993 comedy *Wayne's World*, Mike Meyers (Wayne) dreams he meets Jim Morrison of the Doors. Morrison informs Wayne he is destined to put on a concert. When Wayne asks how he is supposed to get the bands to come, Morrison tells him, "If you book them, they will come."

All you have to do is take the first step and the rest will fall into place. Sometimes taking the first step is all that is necessary to put the rest of the trip into motion.

Whether long or short-term, traveling is simple. Choose a place to go, decide upon your method of getting from point A to point B, and then use said transportation to get to your destination. Aside from the time it takes, the distance between the two points is immaterial. Whether you buy a bus, train, plane, or helicopter ticket, if you buy it, chances are, you'll figure out the rest along the way.

Advocating the purchase of an around the world ticket or moving to a foreign country with little to no funds would be foolish though for however near or far, traveling requires a multitude of decisions and at least a skeletal plan. While for some traveling comes easy, for others, overcoming the apprehension, fear, family issues, or other limiting beliefs is initially the most complicated step. For those willing to take risk, adventures await; a journey into the unknown.

When I moved to Thailand, the time was right. Having traveled to Canada, Mexico, the Bahamas, Great Britain, Belgium and the Netherlands, I had enough international travel experience to feel comfortable moving to the country. Before traveling to Europe, traveling to Asia was something I considered way out of my comfort zone and too much of a hassle. Despite my travels, I grew up sheltered and knew very little about the ways of the world.

"They don't speak English in Thailand, how can I have fun when I can't understand their language and they can't understand mine?" What an amazingly fucked up thought process.

At the time, I was working for myself and making decent money. Although I had created a business and enjoyed working for myself and the business I had created, I wanted less stress and more out of my life.

One of my customers happened to be a frequent visitor of Indonesia. After several long conversations in which he regaled me with stories of bringing back goods to sell to profit from his trip, I began to believe I too could jet halfway around the world. If it worked out, traveling once in a while would become my occupation and I would live happily ever after, with scantily clad Asian girls at my beck and call. Although I was interested in traveling to

Indonesia, I had always wanted to go to Thailand to train in Muay Thai.

The Los Angeles Times ran travel ads every Sunday, and in the course of searching for a decent fare, I came across several companies in need of air couriers. Courier companies use passenger's check-in baggage for their customer's documents and in return allow you to travel for a highly reduced fare. The up side is a cheap fare, the downside is the courier company tells you what time to be at the airport, what time to depart, where to meet their representative in the airport and the date to return. Missing an appointment meant being blacklisted from their company and purchasing a new ticket at full fare. Being late or staying longer is not an option, but flying as a courier was a good gig and it was in my best interest to avoid screwing it up.

After a few days of searching, I found a Los Angeles based courier, Polo Express, and gave them a call. Initially, I had reservations, for flying as a courier almost sounded too good to be true, but after the company's representative answered my lengthy list of questions, I made arrangements to fly to Bangkok a week later. My first ticket, roundtrip from Los Angeles to Bangkok, cost just $200.

In the next year, I traveled to Bangkok four more times, once for $50, and visited Chiang Mai, Chiang Rai, Pattaya, Koh Samet and several other cities. I loved the energy of Bangkok and the laid back, Mai Pen Rai mentality of the Thais. My appetite for the country became insatiable and after the first three trips, my thoughts turned to moving to the country. There was very little holding me back, but I had yet to figure out how to earn a living while on the road.

One day, a light bulb went off, illuminating my path to Thailand. I would sell my business.

Without a profit and loss statement or balance sheet, I somehow finagled a deal with a friend in the printing industry. The business I had started with $500 sold for $34,000. There was still the problem of a continual income, but at least I had a chunk of money to tide me over. The plan was to buy a ticket to Thailand, take a year off from life and get reacquainted with myself, sans stress and the monotony of everyday life. The grind of life had taken its' toll, I felt I was losing touch with who I was, and I needed a break.

The structure of the deal dictated I receive $10,000 up front and a $1000 a month for the next two years. No contract, no banks, no financing, just a handshake and a verbal agreement. Not the brightest move, but I wanted to get on the road and see the world.

As soon as I received the ten grand, I paid $700 for a return ticket from Los Angeles to Bangkok. Before leaving I sold, trashed, and gave away what I didn't want or couldn't carry. With all my worldly possessions in a suitcase, a duffel bag, and a small backpack, and no idea what lay ahead, I jumped on a jet and headed into the unknown.

Perhaps my naiveté allowed me to make the move. Perhaps it was guts, or perhaps stupidity, but whatever the reason, I followed through and moved to Thailand. Where or how I would live, I did not know, but I had money to tide me over, and with any luck, I would figure out how to live in the country before the money ran out.

This was incredibly freeing; however, as I would later learn, no matter where you live, life has its' share of vicissitudes and stressful situations. Sometimes the first step is the most important and most difficult. Getting over the fear of taking that first step ultimately determines if you run in place and go nowhere or forge ahead. If I failed, I could always return home and start over again.

Scott Mallon
Lady Thai

"Ah, women. They make the highs higher and the lows more frequent."

Friedrich Nietzsche, German philosopher

***

I

The kid ordering coffee was speaking loudly, waving his arms up and down as he attempted to make his point to the girl standing beside him. For a moment, I thought of shutting him up with a hard smack to the back of his head, but the prospect of sitting in jail dissuaded me from doing so. He and his fat, zit-faced girlfriend were disturbing everyone in the coffee shop, enthralled in some silly conversation about who had cuter photos in their cell phones.

Maybe they are deaf, I thought, as I turned to throw the pair my dirtiest look.

No effect, they kept blabbing away — loudly.

Then I took a step in their direction and said, "Shut the fuck up already!"

There weren't fazed; they didn't hear me, lost in conversation, completely oblivious to anyone outside of their bubble.

They continued screaming at one another.

"I like the one where I'm standing with Pig-ee," the girl

said, trying to make a cute face. "I am so lovely."

"Yes, you are lovely, but my photo with Nong Jeap's cat is much better. That photo should be in a magazine!"

"No! No way! That cat is ugly! How can you say such a thing?"

"He is so ugly, he's lovely," said the kid. "More lovely than you."

"Are you calling me ugly?" she asked.

The girl stood legs spread shoulder width, rolls of flesh spilling out of her jeans. The pants looked painted on, so tight I was amazed she could fit her massive frame inside of them. Giving her a hard kick to the twat crossed my mind, but her thighs touched all the way from her snatch to her knees and my foot would never have fit. She had no gap and probably spent a fortune on baby powder to keep her legs from chafing.

Maybe a piece of chocolate cake would shut her up.

The kid clearly enjoyed talking, but she easily had him beat both in volume and decibels. The fat bitch didn't even stop to take a breath.

How does the kid deal with her persistent yammering?

Man's zest for life dwindles for a number of reasons, one of which is because women who are constantly talking take the joy out of it. Women who only talk to hear themselves speak tend to be the women people least want to hear.

Before I had the chance to buy fatty a piece of cake though, the pair walked away, still arguing about which one of them had better photographs.

The barista behind the counter gave me a tired look and

fought to muster a smile.

"I'm tired!" she said.

I knew exactly what she meant, but being a polite and proper Thai lady, she would not dare say anything negative about a customer.

Give me a cute, quiet and unassuming chick over a smoking hot broad who likes to flap her gums any day. Women who never shut up tend to talk about frivolous subjects or ask far too many questions.

"Why do you do this?"

"Did you ever?"

"When are you going to…"

"Can I?"

"Will you?"

"Can you"

"Why? How come? What is that supposed that mean?

Oh shut the fuck up already. Can't a man get a little peace and quiet without having to tape his woman's mouth shut?

Silence fat chicks with food and hot ones with a stiff dick. There's enough noise pollution in the world without having to come home to a woman who won't shut up. Whiners and yappers — they get screwed once and shown the door — the quiet ones get to stick around for a while.

Women. No subject conjures up such a wide variety of thoughts and emotions for men as the female species. They shower men with affection, bear their children, provide companionship and stability, help build their homes, love them for unknown reasons and are a source of great joy and great frustration. Women are a blessing and a curse; they break men's hearts, break their balls, make them laugh, make them cry and even prompt some to write poetry and sappy love songs. As sweet, caring and understanding as they can be though, women have the potential to be every bit as ruthless and mercenary as men; despite the risks and the hassles, man's urge to be with them is innate and unstoppable.

II

Making any relationship work is a mixture of luck, timing, tolerance, chemistry, proximity and the ability to understand one another's morals and values, however dissimilar. Add in the exotic flavor of Thailand's culture, the nature and personality of Thai women, and the inability to communicate, and a foreigner in a long-term relationship with Thai woman is a long shot.

Once I settled into my new life in Bangkok, I began compiling a roster of women to date and to sleep with. Anywhere I went, my eyes were open to the possibilities. I did not discriminate; light skin, dark skin, waitresses, 7'11 clerks, office workers, traditional masseuse, happy ending-type masseuse, beer bar girls, and every so often, a bank teller or *Pretty girl*.

In the beginning, having the ability to communicate with Thai women who were unable to speak English was my sole impetus for learning the Thai language. Finding women to have sex with was a game of numbers, and as my Thai improved, so did my numbers. The language always was *a way in* (in more ways than one).

The extent of my game, if you can call it such, went something like this:

"I'm sorry, I don't speak Thai. Do you speak English?"

"No, I am sorry, I no speak English."

"I teach you English, you teach me Thai, okay?"

They would stare into my eyes, scouring my inner being for serious defects like an old woman contemplating the purchase of a used car, trying to determine if I was trustworthy or a lemon. I always promised to be a gentleman and keep the door open while we studied, and most of the time, this was all the reassurance they needed. Must have been my babyface that set them at ease.

Making zero effort to get in their pants almost always worked in my favor, but after one or two lessons we either ended up in the sack or I never saw the girl again. Fuck, suck or get out.

Pick up a Thai language book and learn a handful of basic phrases: hello, goodbye, what is your name, how old are you, you are so beautiful, etc. Twenty or thirty phrases will get you surprisingly far and the mere fact that you are attempting to learn the language is enough to make most Thais smile.

Thai women are the convertible Corvettes of their species; built for fun, born to please, and with the right man, willing to go as fast as humanly possible. Most can charm even the most hard-hearted, pessimistic men, and with a wink, nod, and a quick smile, normal male-female etiquette goes out the window.

Three months into my new life in Thailand, I met

twenty-year-old Noi while having lunch at Pizza Hut. She worked there as a waitress and was a student at Mahidol University. She and her co-worker noticed me staring at her body, thinking impure thoughts, but each time she caught me glancing at her, she smiled. Kid stuff. I knew I was in there,

She had white, smooth skin and a face that belied her innocence; if she were any shorter she could pass for a munchkin from The Wizard of Oz. With heels on she might have been 5'2, but her body was solid, her ass small and round, and her breasts ample. Her breasts were so large she always looked ready to topple over. On our first date, she came wearing a Hello-Kitty t-shirt two sizes too small, bright pink lipstick, silver nail polish and short shorts that allowed a sliver of ass out for the world to enjoy. I got an immediate woody.

Neither of us spoke much, instead we just stared at each other, giggling sporadically. I wondered how long it was going to take us to get naked, hoping it would be sooner than later. My Thai was limited to hello, you are beautiful, go straight, turn left, turn right, stop, how much, and suck my dick. Her English was limited to hello, bye-bye, I like, very good, and no problem. She was perfect.

We went back to my place after dinner, and after an hour of gawking at one another, she was naked and spread eagle on my bed. I stroked her small, overgrown bush for what seemed like an eternity until finally, we had sex.

Barely capable of communicating with one another, she spoke pigeon-English, I spoke crappy Thai. After a brief respite, we had sex again. And again, until eventually the first rays of sunlight crept through the curtains. Only then did we sleep. Hours later we woke up, reached for each other, saying nothing, and had sex again. She didn't leave for three days. For the next six months she came over twice a week without fail to have sex and tidy my room. We usually only went out to bars or to stock up on groceries, never engaged in a serious conversation, never discussed being a couple, and only once did I give her money, 100 baht for taxi fare. She ate constantly though and I spent a pretty penny feeding her.

We would lay around watching TV in my studio apartment, me in my underwear, her in her little girl underwear and bra, tits always falling out. The tits would fall out, I would lick and suck them, and we would end up fucking and sucking until we were completely spent. At night, if we felt like getting out of bed, we would go out to the bar of her choice, meet with her friends, get drunk, and do it all over again.

If we were hungover or feeling especially lazy, which was the norm, we would order room service from the downstairs restaurant. Eat, sleep, shit, shower, and fuck. Eat, sleep, shit, shower and fuck. Life was just how I wanted it to be.

III

Thai men prefer white-skinned Thai women, and in the course of taking me from point A to point B, countless taxi drivers have asked me why this is so.

"Why do foreigners only like dark Thai women?"

"Because they are stupid."

"You don't like dark-skinned Thai women?" he asked.

"I like all women! Dark skin, light skin, it doesn't matter, it's all pink on the inside!"

This always gets a chuckle out of them, nevertheless, they still claim to want a light-skinned Thai girl, not a dark-skinned one. It's engrained in their psyche to make such statements.

I make a weak attempt to enlighten them using logic, "If you have a beautiful, dark-skinned Thai woman laying naked next to you in bed with her legs open, are you going to say, 'Sorry, I need to leave, I only like white-skinned women?'"

Personally, I think they're all full of shit. The power of the vagina is enormous and most taxi drivers would fuck anything with a hole.

On one longer than usual taxi ride, the driver and I began talking about my time in Thailand and my opinion of Thai women.

"My wife is fat and she is not beautiful, but I still love her and love sex with her."

"Well, that's good," I said, startled at how forthcoming he was.

"But she does not like sex."

"Why not?"

"She is always angry with me. She says I am selfish and finish too quickly."

A premature ejaculator — no wonder she's mad — bummer.

"So she never cums?" I ask.

"Nooooo."

"This is a problem," I said, instantly morphing into a male version of Dr. Ruth. "Women want to cum, too. They need it just like you do and you need to last long enough for her to be happy."

"I don't know anything about sex and she is the only woman I have ever been with. I try but it feels so good."

"Well, it's supposed to feel good," I said. "That's why people love sex. Do you eat her pussy?"

"Oh, no, no, no, never."

"Why not?"

He shook his head side to side, disgusted at the thought of putting his face in his wife's most intimate of areas.

"I never," he said, drawing his head back.

"Eat her pussy," I said. "Do it softly. Ask her to tell you when she likes it. I think she will like it very much."

"Really?"

"If you do it softly and she helps you, she's going to like it a lot."

"Maybe I try," he said, the look in his eyes changing as if he were giving the act serious consideration.

Out of the corner of my eye, I noticed him rubbing his crotch. He did so longer than necessary. The guy was getting horny listening to me talk about making *his* wife cum.

Immediately I changed the subject.

"Do you have any children?"

"Three."

"How old?"

"Fifteen, thirteen, and seven."

Several questions later, I arrived at my destination. He thanked me profusely and promised to go home and give his wife's pussy a thorough licking. My contribution to the male species in Thailand.

IV

There are numerous misconceptions about Thailand: you can live like a King for five dollars a day, you never know if a Thai woman is a chick with a dick, the people are all poor and backwards and will rob you any chance they get, and they are all dying to leave their country in pursuit of a green card.

Perhaps one of the most popular misconceptions though, is that all Thai women are whores, gold diggers, and home wreckers. As if these things happen nowhere else on the planet. This generalization is far too broad (excuse the pun) to be accurate, and while there may be a modicum of truth to this, women all over the world want a partner who is financially sound and capable of carrying his own weight and then some. People want and need money and men tend to get into trouble when women shrewdly manipulate their emotions. There is a time and a place to part with money and the trick is learning when to do so. A man normally would not give away his money back home simply because a woman asked him to, so why would he do so anywhere else?

In between one of my first trips to Thailand, I went out to a local watering hole with the intention of finding a lonesome female in dire need of companionship and willing to allow me to use her body as my playground. I stopped a waitress as I entered the joint and ordered a shot of Patron and a Corona. The perfect way to start an evening; down a shot of Tequila, sip the Corona, order another shot of Tequila, down it, sip the Corona, keep the libations flowing. Two hours later, I had done this four times and was drunk. From across the room I spotted a petite young woman with a warm smile and a nice rack. Feeling no inhibitions, I give myself a quick internal pep talk, walk over, and introduce myself.

"Hey, how are you. I'm Scott."

"Nice to meet you, I'm Tracy.

"Are you here alone?" I said.

"Yes, you wanna sit down?"

Things were looking up.

I am drunk, she smells fantastic and I would prefer to fuck her in lieu of going home alone. We share a shot of tequila, then another, and get chummier with each passing second. I like this girl, or at least my prick does, so I ask her to go somewhere quiet.

"How bout we go down the street to TGI Fridays for a late-night snack?"

"Okay, sounds good," she said.

She was drunk too and I can hardly contain myself.

This is almost too good to be true.

Minutes later, we arrive. We walk in, smiles wide, and immediately head for the most intimate booth I can find in the back corner of the restaurant. Our waitress walks over unenthusiastically, and takes our order.

"Can we have an order of onion rings, two Coronas,

and two shots of Patron," I said, slurring my words.

The light is good to my new friend and she is prettier than I thought. Or maybe it's the booze and my hard-on talking.

There is an irresistible wholesomeness to her, but she is aloof, as if she is half here, half somewhere else. Half here is better than not here at all, as long as the part I can have sex with is present.

Can't screw this up. Be cool. Relax, turn on the charm and don't talk too much.

Our legs are intertwined and my dick is painfully hard. Then we kiss and everything and everyone around us disappears. We continue kissing for several minutes, our bodies growing increasingly hot. I am ready to pay the bill.

Then she pulls away.

"I can't," she says.

"What's the matter?" I ask, confused. "Are you married?"

"No, no, I'm single. It's not that."

"Then what?"

"It's not you, it's me."

Oh no, not the it's not you, it's me, line. What's next, let's be friends?

I wait patiently for her answer, wondering what happens next as my cock deflates.

Unsure of what to do, I say nothing. So close, yet so far.

In an instant, the details of her life come rushing out.

Mom is sick — pancreatic cancer. The disease is spreading quickly and it won't be long now. Dad had a heart attack and passed away two years ago and now she has no one to take care of her. Mom no longer has health insurance and she recently lost the house. Tracy is her only caregiver, the one person left to take care of her. Trouble is, if Tracy is taking care of Mom, she can't work full-time. There is very little money and they are both waiting for Mom to die.

Fuck, I liked her better when she didn't talk.

I listen intently, wanting to care, but shocked at my bad luck.

"Wow, I'm sorry. I don't know what to say."

Does this mean I'm not getting laid? Can I have a quick BJ in the restroom?

Tracy is sweet and charming and her sincerity and situation are overwhelming. I'm inebriated and horny and I'm having a hard time thinking of anything else. By the time Tracy finishes telling her story, the poor girl is practically in tears.

"I came out and wanted to get smashed. I thought it would help, but I don't know what we're going to do."

"We have lost so much," said Tracy. "I can't believe it."

"I'm sure it will work out," I said, lying. I press my cock against her.

"I've been paying all the bills from my savings, but I am running out of money. The bills are due at the end of the month and I don't know what I'm going to do."

Pussy starved and pussy whipped, I am willing to say almost anything and blurt out, "Maybe I can help."

Sucker! You are no longer a love interest, you are her ATM.

This is the most inappropriate response a man with any

18

balls could give. Sure, there is chemistry and definitely something magical happening. This magical feeling is lust. Even if a woman in this sort of situation is genuine, why would I give away my hard earned money? She is a stranger and I have no idea if she is telling the truth or not.

Her eyes open wide and she lifts her head.

"How can you help me?"

Damn, why did I say that? She probably would have fucked me anyway.

Saying no makes life so much easier.

I change tact.

"You could babysit my kids for me," I say, desperate to get out of the situation. "My house needs cleaning. I could pay you."

The look on her face immediately changes and moments later, we bid one another farewell.

I never see her again and I go home with blue balls.

She went home with no money. Close, but no cigar honey.

Giving or loaning money to a woman you just met is out of the question. How often do men in the western world hand over money to a woman back home? Thai men do not do this either, unless the woman is a prostitute, so why is it when a foreigner comes to Thailand, the situation is different? This subject shouldn't have to be discussed, but more than a few extremely successful, good-looking guys have pissed their money away because they're too soft-hearted to *say no*.

A man has three choices if a woman is after his cash; tell her to get lost, put her to work, or give her what she wants. Either way, no one is forcing the man to empty his wallet.

In the popular TV sitcom, Seinfeld, Jerry's outlook towards his relationships with women is almost perfect. When he hooks up with a good-looking woman, of course, he's happy. If he has problems with her, he then debates whether or not the problems are worth dealing with and if it is time to move on. If a girl bails on him, for whatever reason, he simply shakes his head and gets on with life. He cares more about himself than anyone else, and while it may sound selfish, this is about the best attitude you can have with women, regardless of their looks, sexual prowess, nationality or financial standing.

V

Much like the Netherlands accepts the use of marijuana and hashish, Thailand tolerates prostitution and a decreasing number of women still allow philandering to a degree. Asian women are well aware of the wandering tendencies of men and would rather have their man go to a prostitute for a few hours of sex than have them involved in an ongoing love affair with a woman who may steal their husband.

It pays to be cautious and know the woman's position on the issue; there are numerous recorded instances of an irate Thai wife slicing off her husband's pecker then feeding it to a duck waddling in the vicinity. Hence the Thai phrase, "Give the dick to the duck."

One can never be sure how a Thai woman will react to their partner's transgressions on any given day, and for the cheating male, it pays to be judicious.

They Call Me Farang

The media and naysayers of prostitution would have you believe foreign men come to Thailand to take advantage of Thai women, as if they were shriveling violets, unable to ward off the advances of the devil-male from the western world. Poor impoverished Thai girls, naïve to the ways of the world, fall prey to fat, ugly men unable to land a woman in their own country. These dastardly men only desire underage women who will fulfill their perverted sexual fantasies. Of course, attractive men would never dream of using ladies for hire. What a crock of shit.

Given the opportunity to work a more mainstream job, most whores will choose to remain loyal to the bar. Leaving the bar means less money, less freedom, and no more staying up all night and sleeping all day.

Men led by their dicks prowl the beer bars and go-go's of Bangkok, testosterone seeping into the night, searching patiently and impatiently for their next conquest. There are two types of men, lions and lambs. The lion sits back and does what he wants, when he wants, without concern for the girls in the bars. He knows they need him more than he needs them and there is no need to run after them. They will come, after all, if a woman wants to engage in sex, she will let you know. The lamb goes after any woman who gives him the time of day, following their rhythm, doing what they want without thinking about themselves. They are prey and fall victim to any woman who wants to take advantage of them.

Complete with flashing lights and an abundance of scantily clad women, Nana Entertainment Plaza resembles the seediest area of Las Vegas condensed into a three-story, 100 x 100 yard square packed with beer bars and go-go's. The scent of vagina is everywhere, thick and pungent, and *The Girl* is out there, waiting to accommodate the man with money who finds her, ready for the adventure that comes with the business. Every girl is *'The Girl'*.

The vast majority of Thai prostitutes service Thai clientele, although the Thai establishments tend to be more discreet than the in-your-face action of Pattaya, Soi Cowboy, Patpong, or Nana Plaza. Try telling this to some Debbie Do-gooder though and your words will fall on deaf ears.

VI

Another of the young women I was with at the beginning of my stay in Bangkok was Joy, a 22-year old from Khon Khaen. We had been seeing each other for a month, nothing serious, but we were fond of one another and made each other laugh. It was obvious she had spent time around foreigners; her English was better than average and any time she spoke English it was easy to detect British and Australian accents.

One day while we were walking down Sukhumvit Road, a thirty-something, unkempt white woman with stringy hair walked up to us and initiated the usual pleasantries.

"Hi Joy, how are you?" asked the girl.

"I'm fine, thank you. How are you?"

"I'm good. What's happening?"

"We were just walking around. Probably go get something to eat, why?"

"Are you okay? I mean, really?"

"I'm okay."

I immediately disliked this girl and sensed the feeling was mutual.

"Honey, I need to go to the pharmacy," said Joy.

The moment Joy was out of sight, the woman stepped towards me and said, "You're fucking her, aren't you? You pig."

Stunned, I said nothing, wondering why this crazy bitch wanted to know what I was doing with Joy.

"You know, it can't be easy for her. Sleeping with men for money."

"She hasn't asked me for any money and I'm not paying her," I said. "Mind your own business, ya rotten cunt."

Her jaw dropped, I smiled, did a quick 180, and walked into the pharmacy.

"Everything okay, honey?"

"Yea, fine. Who is that bitch?"

"She help me before."

When we walked outside, the girl was gone. Turns out this broad worked for a Christian NGO whose goal was to help Thai women stop prostituting themselves. Joy hit a bad streak in her life and became a freelancer at Nana Disco. The woman's organization had given her a couple of bags of groceries and from then on, she would show up every so often at Joy's apartment trying to convert her to Christianity. Joy, like the majority of Thais was a Buddhist though, and refused to become a Christian. Anytime the girl showed up, Joy was polite, but becoming a born-again was the last thing she wanted. Joy and I stopped seeing each other not long after the encounter. One day I stopped going to see her and that was the end of our fling.

VII

Women work in bars to earn more than they would earn working in a factory, selling fruit, or sweating in a rice field, and while meeting their future ex-husband while working as a prostitute might be one of their dreams, chances are they are selling their bodies to me, you, Tom, Dick, Harry, Jerry, Larry, Curly, Moe, Somchai and anyone else for the money. First and foremost, it's about the money. If she is a working girl, she is not your girl, she's just your turn.

If the woman wants money, anybody could be the guy. If you have more money than she does and are willing to part with some of it, you are the answer, at least until she finds a bigger, better deal.

The Golden Rule: Do not get emotionally involved with a prostitute.

Would James Bond fall in love with a prostitute? No, he would take the time to know them sexually, pay them and leave. No need to get sentimental.

If you ever begin to feel your prostitute of the day is different, run, hide, ask a friend to smack you over the head, do whatever you can to distance yourself from her. She may actually like you, but the odds are that she needs money more and for her at least, money and family take precedence over her immediate feelings. Without delay, change bars, change women, and move on to the next woman.

There will always be desperate, idiotic men who know nothing about Thailand willing to make a whore their girlfriend or wife. They truly believe their lady is different from every other whore; maybe so, but paying as you go is far less problematic. When a tourist comes to Thailand, falls in love with a working girl in a matter of days, then makes plan to marry her, save her, and whisk her away to the safety and comfort of his native land, he's a codependent Captain Save-a-Ho.

If a man falls madly in love with a bar girl, then goes through all the trouble of bringing her back to his home country, this in itself is a monumental ordeal. Finally, he brings her back, and the two can start their lives together. When his friends learn he met her in a Pattaya brothel, their respect for him will plummet as fast as it takes him to tell them.

Maybe it doesn't matter – but it should.

Everything is hunky dory at first. He is certain he has found the woman of his dreams. Mom, Dad, Grandma, Grandpa and the entire family like her; she genuinely cares about you (so you think) and she is a sweet, caring, loving young woman. One evening, you take her to a family gathering. Predictably, everyone loves her. The drinks flow freely and everyone is having a great time. You turn around to find your sweet little honey shit-face drunk, dancing on Mom and Dad's coffee table holding on to an imaginary pole.

When you brought your dream girl back with you, you explained to her that you were poor and life was a struggle.

"Honey, no problem, I only want your love."

Anything is better than living in her horrible, wretchedly poor country and she's eternally grateful you came into her life and rescued her. As long as she has you, this is all that is important. Hogwash.

Millions of people around the world live in poverty. Many are happier and more content than those who are well off financially. Just because she is poor doesn't mean you are her savior and she will be forever grateful. Poor, homeless and starving is much different from having no money in the bank because she feels compelled to build a house, buy a cell phone and gold necklaces, and pay off Ma-ma's Isuzu pickup truck.

When your sweet little muffin-pie finally realizes life in your country is no better than life in Thailand, she might decide to hatch a plan to move on to greener pastures — without you. Then you find out she's been having midday rendezvous with your neighbor. Your best buddy tells you she offered him a blowjob for $25. You're shocked, devastated and heartbroken. Why? How could she do such a thing?

Did you really expect to turn a whore into a housewife?

Working girls are not regular girls, no matter how regular they seem. They may give you a girlfriend experience (GFE) but they are not prostituting themselves because you're handsome – even if you are - they are doing so because they're willing to sell their time and bodies for much needed income. This brings us back to the golden rule; do not get emotionally involved with a working girl. You wouldn't do so back home and it's no different elsewhere.

The prostitute knows the interaction is a business transaction. If given the chance, the more intelligent women turn the transaction into a pseudo love affair, thus maximizing their potential long-term earnings. Customers know this too, however, the line between game and reality is all too often blurred. When a business engagement becomes love, pseudo or otherwise, this is when problems occur.

There are women who act as if they are above being a prostitute. You can find them in places like the Hard Rock Café, Rivas, Spassos, and RCA. They play it off as if they are just girls out for a good time, and they very well might be, but the truth is they are putting on a front. They are working girls, out for your cash.

Go home with one of these women and in the morning, she might just have her hand out for taxi fare. This in itself isn't a bad thing, after all, giving a woman cab fare is the gentlemanly thing to do after you've gotten to know her inside and out. Cab fare is only a couple of baht though; if she asks for a thousand baht, or more, you can be certain they are "on the game." Decent Thai women tend to only ask for money once you're in an established relationship.

So how are men supposed to understand women and carry on healthy relationships? Think with the big head, not the little one, and whatever the little head thinks you should do, do exactly the opposite. After all, life's a crapshoot.

Scott Mallon

Jerseys

"Corruption is everywhere, but it prospers here."
Sergey Veremeenko, Russian Oligarch

***

Poverty often necessitates an "at any cost" mentality. In third world countries, where police officers only make a few hundred dollars a month, or less, bribery and corruption are the cogs in the wheels of justice. In theory, corruption is a huge negative; on a small scale, a $10 payment to a traffic cop saves you the headache of going to court. In serious matters, corruption and bribery can be your best friend, helping to avoid jail time.

When I decided to move to Thailand, I planned to come for a year. I would train in Muay Thai, travel through Southeast Asia in a quest for an adventure, and get to know myself again without stress. Once the time off had recharged my batteries, I would move back to the US and start life afresh. When the year ended though, I decided to stay another month, then three more months, until finally, I decided to stay. Another year passed and I ran out of money.

After researching the best cities to work and live, I decided on Seattle. Within a month, I landed on a fishing boat in the middle of the Bering Sea. After six months, I had saved enough to give Thailand another try. Three days after reaching port, I hopped on a plane bound for Thailand.

They Call Me Farang

A month after arriving, I started exporting Thai goods through eBay and a poorly built website. Silk, Saa paper, photo albums, cotton tinsel pillows, fisherman's pants, semi-precious stones, painted serpentine eggs, chopsticks, pewter; if it came from Asia and I thought it would sell, I would throw a photo of the product online, cross my fingers, and pray it sold.

Eventually, the desire to buy anything I could make a buck off led me to a row of shop houses across the street from the National Stadium in the Pathumwan area of Bangkok. While in a taxi one morning, I noticed several shops displaying football jerseys in their windows. Each shop had different quality jerseys and for the next two hours I went shop to shop inspecting them. Some of the shops had counterfeit rugby jerseys, others had cheap football jerseys costing two-three dollars, and several had football jerseys that were such high quality I thought they were authentic.

Thai stores and street merchants sell a wide variety of counterfeit products; everything from Rolex watches to Nike shoes to Prada handbags. At the time, I had no idea that the sale of football jerseys and related products around the world were so massive.

Growing up in the US, I knew European football as soccer. My knowledge of the sport was zilch. When I saw the jerseys, I sensed an opportunity and bought a dozen of the most popular jerseys. Then, I took photos of them and began selling them online. Forty-eight hours later, I purchased 150 more. Those sold in a week. For the first time since moving to Thailand, with sales snowballing and the money pouring in, I had a regular income stream and money to burn. In a few weeks, I learned everything I needed to know about jerseys.

Sellers on eBay sold the jerseys as authentic replicas, but the semantics of calling an unlicensed, Thai-made jersey an authentic replica is nothing more than trickery. A jersey is either an authentic jersey or an authentic replica, licensed and made by reputable manufacturers or it's an unauthorized fake.

Selling phony watches and handbags crossed my mind, but for some reason, the thought of doing so rubbed me the wrong way. Selling phony football jerseys seemed acceptable, selling Rolex watches and Gucci handbags did not.

By the fourth month, sales approached a thousand jerseys a month. In the beginning, I had been content selling jerseys retail through eBay for $49. The jersey's cost $5.50 a jersey so the markup was excellent. Then wholesaler buyers began buying 100-200 jerseys at a time, paying $15-$20 per jersey. The orders kept coming and the money kept rolling in. To make certain I always had enough stock, I began special ordering the best-selling jerseys by the dozen, sometimes even a hundred at a time.

The shops I dealt with only sold the highest quality jerseys. Prior to selling the jerseys, $2000 was a good month; once I began selling them, I earned this much in a week. The money was coming in faster than I could count, but it flew out of my hands just as fast. The majority of the time, my daily routine never varied: wake up, have sex with a girl from the previous evening, send her on her way, work for three hours, go to the post office, have lunch, and then welcome another woman into my not-so-humble abode.

It soon became impossible to source enough jerseys to fill orders; demand was too great for the supply. While in Singapore on a visa run, I stumbled upon Peninsula Plaza. The shopping center sells a variety of items, authentic football jerseys and sports equipment being among them. The prices of the jerseys left room to earn a profit so I bought two dozen, flew back to Thailand, sold them, and then flew back with a wad of cash to buy more. Every two weeks, I would fly to Singapore, buy two hundred jerseys, throw them in a duffel bag and suitcase, then bring them back into Thailand. Duty-free, of course.

Some jerseys cost as much as $35-$40, most ran $25-$30. The more I bought, the better the price the stores gave me. The cost of traveling to Singapore ate away most of the profit, but I averaged out the cost per jersey including the travel expenses, then mixed in authentic with the fakes. Once Singapore became a regular gig, I developed a basic website and started selling the jerseys for $54.95 to $69.95 each. The same price as licensed, authentic jerseys. Purchasing authentic jerseys in Singapore gave me legitimacy, but I was making less money and at least fifty-percent of my product line was still bogus.

Several of the wholesale buyers began questioning whether the jerseys were authentic and I had a hard time flat out lying, instead telling them that at as far as I knew, I was selling genuine, authentic replica jerseys, made in Thailand. More semantics.

The sale of the jerseys had peaked and my partying

needed to stop. My drinking and carousing were taking their toll and feeling like shit had become normal. The more money I earned, the less I slept and the worse I felt.

Then, through a mutual friend, I met Beau, the woman who would later become my wife.

As a full-time student with a full-time job, she had no time to waste. Go to school, go to work, come home, do the laundry, in bed by nine. Within six months she had graduated; I was still trying to regain my focus. With a busy life of her own and higher priorities than dating, it would take two months before we went out on our first date. Even then, it was only with a group of friends. With several women on the hook, none of whom I considered special, I was in no hurry to get into a serious relationship. A month would pass before we would go out again. This time though, we went out alone and something clicked. Before I knew it, we were in a relationship.

Desperate to legitimize and keep my business afloat, I began selling authentic, football-related products such as clocks, towels, anything I could find. Selling authentic meant an even lower profit margin, but it meant going legit and having a sustainable business.

My trips to the bars slowed. Never one to buy alcohol or drink at home, I stopped drinking and started keeping more reasonable hours. Then Beau asked if I wanted to move into her apartment. After paying rent, electric, water, internet, and maid service, the cost of living in my apartment was almost $2000, at the time, approximately 80,000 baht. We already spent most of our free time together, so I packed up and moved in with her, further distancing myself from the nightlife and breaking the party cycle once and for all.

Late one afternoon, while napping, the room began to shake, awakening me. An earthquake in Thailand? Over and over again, someone's fist slammed against the door. Eager to find out who had the audacity to pound away at our door, I leaped up and turned the doorknob.

A pack of fifteen plainclothes police officers pushed their way inside the room.

"Mr. Scott? Scott Mallon?" asked one officer.

"Yes."

The officer stepped through the door, turned to his right, then walked over to the armoire where a few hundred jerseys were visibly overflowing. Manchester United, Liverpool, Arsenal, Brazil, England, Argentina; I stocked just about every professional team in existence. The officer picked up one of the jerseys, held it in the air for me to see, turned and smiled.

A special internet task force had been tracking my burgeoning online enterprise.

"You sell football shirt," he said, continuing to smile. "You sell copy."

"I bought them in Thailand," I said. "I thought they were real."

He thrust a pack of documents into my face.

"You know they are copy."

"Why don't you arrest the people who sold them to me?"

I already knew the answer to the question. Every month, the owners of the jersey shops paid tea money to the police. How was I sure? One of the shop owners had complained it was hard to make money with the police regularly stopping by to pick up their 200,000-baht monthly fine.

This is Thailand.

"You can take care problem," said one of the officers. "You pay money."

"How much."

"400,000 baht," he said.

$10,000 USD.

"I don't have that kind of money," I said.

Thoughts of all the money pissed away on hookers and booze quickly turned into thoughts of rotting in the Bangkok Hilton.

"Okay, you go police station," he said.

"Can I make a phone call?"

My only link to the outside world, the cell phone.

"No problem," he said.

Not wanting anyone to hear my conversation, I opened the sliding glass door and walked out to our 3' x 3' balcony. Jumping from the fourteenth floor would be painful, but it was the only option of escape. For a split second, I thought of a dramatic suicide. However, reality slapped my face before I could do so.

Going splat on the asphalt is way too painful.

With great pain and some hesitation, I dialed my parent's number in Florida. Immediately, my mother knew something was not right.

"What's wrong?"

"The police just showed up at my door," I said.

"The police!" she said, gasping. "Why? What did you do?"

"I didn't do anything."

If you didn't do anything, why are they there?"

"Well, I was selling football shirts... fake ones."

"They're going to throw you in jail for that?" she asked.

"They want 400,000 baht or they say I'm going to jail for two years."

Silence.

"Mom?"

"Why do you get yourself into these predicaments? That's a lot of money!"

"I know. Especially since I don't have it," I said.

"We're not going to give you $10,000. Talk to them and see what you can do," she said. "It will all work out."

"Okay," I said, not quite believing her.

"They're just trying to shake you down. Figure out what you can do and let me know," she said. "What on earth were you thinking?"

"Making money."

The thing about money is it doesn't matter how much you make, what matters most is the amount you keep.

The police took my computer, monitor, and all of the jerseys and drove me to the police station. Upon arrival, an officer pointed to a chair at a large table in a conference room.

"Farang. Sit down. One moment."

One aspect of the Thai justice system I have never understood was the photographing of a suspect pointing at whatever items they were selling or possessing.

"Take a photo."

Pointing to the shirts, I look at the photographer and give my shittiest grin.

Then I asked Beau for my phone.

"Get me out of here," I said.

"I'll try."

An officer put his hand on my shoulder and led me to a holding cell where two guards were waiting my arrival.

"Sawasdee Khup," one of them said, in Thai.

"Sawasdee Khup…"

Struggling, I managed a weak smile.

"Oh, you can speak Thai."

"Yes," I said, nodding.

"Big deal," I thought. "I can speak Thai. A lot of good it's doing me now."

"We leave the door open," he said, grinning. "But do not run away."

Pacing in and out of the cell, the hours passed and I still had no idea what was transpiring on the outside.

In the lobby of the police station, Beau tried negotiating my release, however, the disparity between the 400K baht the police desired and the 20,000 baht she was willing to part with was unacceptable. The police controlled my freedom and knew they had me; now they would extract as much money as they could and it would take more than 20,000 baht to get them to budge.

At this moment, I learned another valuable lesson; never put yourself in a position where the police have a valid reason to throw you in jail. Sounds like something I should have learned when I was in kindergarten, but in

Thailand, it is more complicated than this.

"You, farang, come with me," said the guard.

One of our best friends, Stephan, now stood in the middle of the lobby arguing with a fat detective about the value of the bust.

Knowing Stephan to be a smooth talker who had experience with the police, Beau called him, told him of the dilemma, and he was now working his magic.

"You know, he not sell many," said Stephan. "No big money."

Although he spoke passable Thai, he would speak pigeon-English with them anytime he could get away with it.

"We understand you have a job to do and know he must pay. But if you ask for big money, maybe you get nothing."

Then, with great theatrics, Stephan pulled out his 6-inch biker wallet, dug around for several seconds, and pulled out a laminated card. Holding it by the edges as if it were a million-dollar photograph, he turned to the detective and smiled.

"If Scott goes to jail, I call big lawyer, my friend. He will take care Scott," he said, handing the detective the card.

"If I call him, nobody happy."

"How much he can pay?" asked the detective.

"One hundred thousand baht."

The detective stared at him, looking for a sign of weakness, then he turned and looked at Beau, and finally, at me.

"Okay, you have money?"

"We can give you this now," she said.

Out came an envelope.

"This is 20,000 baht. We can go to the bank and get the rest tomorrow morning, she said."

"This no problem," said Stephan.

"He has baby, he stay Thailand long time already. He not run away."

The detective nodded in agreement.

"One moment," he said.

When he came back, he gave me three sheets of paper.

"You sign."

The document was in Thai, so I turned it over to Beau for the once-over.

"You need to give them the money tomorrow," she said. "If you don't, they will put you in jail and you must go to court. Also, if they catch you selling jerseys again, they will put you in jail."

"Okay," I said.

Under the circumstances, I would have agreed to just about anything. I just wanted to get out of there as fast as I could. The inside of a Thai prison was the last place I wanted to see.

The next day, we went to the bank and withdrew 15,000 baht, all the cash I had. Unbeknownst to me, Stephan had agreed to loan us the remaining 65,000 baht.

Just before noon, we walked into the police station. Upon seeing us, the detective greeted us like old friends.

"Sawasdee khup!" he said. "Nice to see you."

I put forth the most authentic phony smile I could muster and as I handed him the money, asked, "Okay, now no more problem, right?"

"Thieving cocksucker," I thought to myself.

"No problem," he said, laughing.

I only had myself to blame, nevertheless I was seething inside. A hundred thousand baht, down the toilet. Looking in his eyes, I fought hard to control my disdain, instead smiling as if I were his best friend.

So this is what it is like being Thai, I thought. This is how they play the game. This is The Killing Smile.

Never again would I underestimate the power of money.

The officer thrust another stack of papers in my face.

"Sign paper," he said.

Without looking at him, I signed, and then pushed the papers across the table.

Right on cue, another officer walked out with my computer and the jerseys, set them on the table, turned around and headed to the back of the station.

Free at last. Free at last.

The police returned all the jerseys, but as soon as we got home, Beau had me throw them in the dumpster outside our apartment. Another flush of the toilet.

"Never again," she said.

Scott Mallon
Ninety Grand

"Waste your money and you're only out of the money, but waste your time and you've lost part of your life."

Michael LeBoeuf, American Author

***

Picturesque beaches, stunning temples, world renowned nightlife, and an exotic, laid-back lifestyle are but a few of the reasons why Thailand attracts millions of visitors each year. The irresistible charm of Thai women is another of the reasons.

As one of the most visited countries on the planet, Thailand is also a premier expat haven.

From the first time Terry set foot in Thailand, he had one goal, to sleep with as many women as possible. An insatiable predator, he hit on women everywhere he went, no shame in his game. Whenever in the proximity of a woman, Terry assessed the situation, first checking out her demeanor, then the body from head to toe. Always on the lookout for an opportunity to get laid, he couldn't help himself. If a woman was halfway decent, he had to stop and make a play.

"It's all a game of numbers," he would say. "I'll never get laid waiting for them to open their legs."

Walking along in the midst of a serious conversation, he would stop to work his magic.

"Gimme a minute."

A minute turned into fifteen, and then afterward, good or bad, he would force me to listen to every minute detail of what transpired. One of his most annoying habits came after he slept with one of the women. His non-stop bragging and talk of his dick size got tiresome.

"Dude, last night I made this chick see Buddha."

Even more irritating was that he would tell me the details of his liaison in the middle of a restaurant or store.

"I had her squealing like a pig!" he would say, laughing. "Ohhhh, Terry, Terry! Dick big big. You number one for me!"

"Ugghhhhhhh, shut up already!"

"They don't call me Big Terry for nothing."

Every night he visited the red light districts, a woman for pay on each arm or on his lap, drinking and partying until inebriated. Discos and go-go's were his first preference, then beer bars and massage parlors, but in the end, all that mattered was living a life of supreme debauchery.

"I'm gonna have a dozen naked chicks running around my house servicing me anytime I want."

"Uh huh, sure ya are."

All it took was one drunken, sex-filled night on

the town and Terry was making plans for a return trip.

Before moving to Thailand, Terry worked as a software developer in Southern California, clearing $150K a year. Expensive designer clothing, Rolex watches, flashy jewelry and a leased Porsche were his norm. With money to burn and little debt, by most standards, he was living the life. Single by choice, but was rarely alone, he was the ultimate narcissistic personality.

Thirty-something Delta Airlines reservations agent Jay lived on the outskirts of Washington DC. After several conversations on the WSA, an online forum dedicated to men who travel around the world for exotic pussy, the two began talking on Skype, and soon, they found themselves making arrangements to go to Thailand together.

A self-professed part-time Thailand resident, Jay actually was only able to travel as often as he did because he worked for Delta. All he had to do was pay the tax on the price of a ticket, put in a request to fly standby, and jump on the jet.

A day after the dynamic duo arrived, Jay introduced me to Terry. We spent the next week bar hopping and chasing tail. A search for the perfect whore. First stop on the circuit, the Beer Garden, an indoor-outdoor bar full of filthy sluts, but nevertheless, worth a look. If you were patient, every so often you could find a cutie just off the farm. Most of the time the place was full of old hags. I almost always went after the bartenders behind the bar, which took more time, patience, and after hour drinking. Then it would be off to Nana Plaza, Patpong, Soi Cowboy, or some other den of iniquity, sometimes with several ladies in tow. Male bonding at its finest in the sleaze pits of The Big Mango.

Jay and Terry were both narcissists. Jay thought he was more handsome than he actually was, but in Thailand, women decide if you're handsome or not by the amount of money you have at your disposal. The more money women perceive you to have, the better looking you become. Even though he paid his whores, his narcissism prevented him from accepting that they only wanted his money. He refused to believe he was anything less than a handsome man. In his delusional mind, he was a lady's man; I thought of him as a wannabe playboy whose gift of gab was second-rate, at best.

One day, while waiting to cross Sukhumvit Road to Soi Nana, I asked him if he truly believed he was handsome.

"Do you really think you're like Brad Pitt handsome and that's why the whores like you? I mean, you are paying them."

For the next 30 minutes, he ignored me. Offended by my question, he pouted. I could not stop laughing. We never spoke about his looks again.

Jay earned $1800 a month working for Delta

and while at home in the US, he lived a frugal lifestyle. His routine never changed; wake up, go to work, come home, have dinner and a glass of wine, have an online chat with a Thai or Filipino girl, then go to sleep. It was a frugal, boring existence, but by the time it was time for his next excursion, he had saved enough to stay in a decent hotel.

"Gotta play the part," he would say.

Jay tried to play the part of a big spender, but prying money from his hands was like carving diamonds from a mountain with a rubber knife. He sought acceptance of his frugality, which I never gave him. The truth was I thought he was a cheap cunt; all show and no substance.

On his second trip, Terry began talking about moving to Bangkok. One trip to Thailand is never enough, twice is sufficient to spark the desire to call it home. Upon returning home to what he called 'his mundane existence,' he made *The Decision* and I got *The Call*.

"You've been there a while now. You think you could help me start an online business?" he asked.

"You got money?"

"A little more than $100,000," he said.

"Really? Shit, I'm impressed. The way you live I would have thought you were broke. Sure, I can give you a little help."

All it took was a few words of encouragement and a week later, he quit his job, put everything he owned in storage, and purchased a ticket to Thailand. He was moving to Thailand to start an online export business —*Made in Thailand*. The name made no sense to me because a fair number of the products sold in Thailand originated in China and the name limited his product line. Every year, hundreds of thousands of foreigners with love in their eyes and dreams of a different life try moving to Thailand. Few succeed, at least for the long term, and even with my help, I had my doubts. Terry had only seen the inside of the Nana Plaza go-go bars, Nana Disco, the Hard Rock Cafe, and Patpong, yet despite knowing next to nothing about the country, the culture and the people, he was adamant about starting a business.

"I'm sick of doing the same thing every day. I feel like a robot! I have enough money to live in Thailand for ten years, so what have I got to lose?"

"Your money, that's what. It's up to you," I said. "$100K is not going to last you for ten years, believe me." Although $100,000 was a nice chunk of change, he would be lucky if it lasted 4-5 years.

I had heard it all before, in fact, every time I went out to the bars, at least one drunken fool, usually with a bar girl wrapped around him like an anaconda, slobbering in his ear, would tell me how he was moving to Thailand.

"This place is great! I gotta move here!"

"Right, how do you plan on paying the bills?"

"Look at her man! She's gorgeous."

She's gorgeous, but she'll be a pain in the ass at some point. Believe it pal. Living your life for a woman is a set-up for disappointment, especially for a prostitute. When the money goes, so goes the whore with it.

Terry and I arranged to meet the day after he arrived.

I put together a two-page checklist prioritizing what I thought he needed to do to get his business started and to be successful.

We met for coffee around the corner from Nana Plaza. Terry had yet to find an apartment and was staying at The Majestic.

"You need to find an apartment," I said. "I've written down the names of a couple of areas for you to look."

"Thanks man."

"I also wrote down the names of a couple of places I want you to check out," I said. I wanted him to go to Chatuchak, Prathunam, Prathumwan, and Bobay. He could ask the vendors questions and buy samples of their products.

"Now go out and do what you have to do. Get laid, enjoy yourself and call me once you find an apartment."

"Okay, sounds good."

"If you want me to go with you, I will, but it's gonna cost you. I got my own shit to do."

"I can do it. Thanks for your help, though. I'll

call you."

"In your downtime, go online and do some research on Thai-made goods."

Two weeks went by before he finally called.

"I'm ready," he said. "What do you think I should do first?" he asked.

"Did you do what I told you to do?"

Silence.

I had given him a list of things to do:

1. Figure out the products you want to offer

2. Decide on a name for the business (preferably *not* Made in Thailand)

3. Check to see if the web URL is available

4. Sign up on eBay

5. Register for a PayPal account

6. Get a merchant account and credit card processor

Figuring out what to sell was important. We had discussed this several times, but he could never decide. Now it was imperative he decide.

"I don't know what to sell. I just wanna make money."

"C'mon man, you know that's not good enough."

When it came to becoming an online merchant, he was brain dead.

"There's so many things you can sell: knickknacks, jewelry, Benjarong, furniture, Saa paper, silk. All it takes is one or two items to sell well and you'll earn enough to pay the bills.

"I know, but I don't know what's gonna sell." he said.

"Alright, here's the deal. Budget $5000 for a month of traveling around the country," I said. "Set aside $2500 of this for test products; choose carefully, you don't have to spend it all. Start in Bangkok, then work your way up to Udonthani and over to Chiang Mai. You'll have 2500 for your travel expenses. This should be more than enough."

"But I don't speak Thai," said Terry. "I don't know."

"So then hire me to travel around with you."

"Fifty-thousand baht plus expenses is too much," he said, whining.

"That's my price. I'm worth it."

"Nah, I'll do it on my own. I think I can handle it," he said.

"Money is the international language. All you need to worry about is finding decent products to sell and getting good prices."

"I guess. I'll give it a try."

I didn't hear from him for two months. He never called me and when I called him, his phone was off or he never answered. I thought he was looking for products for his website. Then I got the call.

"I'm in Pattaya. I met a girl," he said.

"Where?"

"In Bangkok. At Nana Disco."

"You fucking bone head. What did I tell you?"

Silence.

"I know, man. Now she's driving me crazy," he said.

"Did you find anything to sell? Have you finished everything on the list?"

"No," he said, giggling like a scolded child.

"You gotta be kidding me."

Thailand's nightlife and women were getting the better of him and he was no closer to starting his business than when he first arrived.

"She's so sweet and nice when we're together," he said. "But I don't understand her. She's not like the chicks back home."

"She's not like the chicks back home because she's Thai," I said, frustrated with his inability to understand such a simple concept.

Those on the path of self-destruction only notice their destination once it's too late to turn back.

"Your money is not going to go as far as you think. Get rid of her before it's too later," I said, pleading with him.

Mired in relationship drama, caught up in passion, he had lost focus. Doing business was the last thing on his mind.

I tried selling him on the idea that once the business was fully functioning and earning him a few dollars, he would be in a better place financially and emotionally. Then he would be thinking more clearly and could look for a relationship-worthy woman.

As soon as my words reached his ears though, he copped an attitude.

"You don't know this girl," he said. "She's helped me a lot."

"Fuck man, the only thing she's done is help keep your pipes clean and siphon your money. What was the one thing I told you?"

Silence.

"Don't get emotionally involved with a working girl!"

"I know, I know," he said, sheepishly.

"You said you wanted to start up a business here. Having some slut to worry about is only going to distract you."

I knew all I had to know from what little he told me. His new love interest worked as a freelancer prostitute at Angel's Disco inside the Nana Hotel. Decent Thai women would never venture inside the place.

"She's not a hooker," he said. "She just goes there to hang out with her friends.

"Bullshit. Stop lying to me and to yourself. How long did it take you to bang her? Be honest."

"Well, the first night. But I didn't pay her!" he said, defensively.

"You're paying her now though, aren't you?"

"I'm helping her," he said.

"Believe me, you are better off cutting her

loose. Then you can focus on your business and cut your expenses."

Did he listen? Of course not. Rarely does anyone listen. Sucked in and slowly sucked dry, he had reached the point where he thought she was the girl of his dreams, and of course, she was different. Nine long months passed before he contacted me again. I called him now and then, but like before, he never answered his phone, or it was always off. Finally, I gave up. The Big Mango had him in its grasp. When I finally did hear from him, he wasted no time telling me he was moving back home.

"It's a great place to party and I love the women, but I don't think I want to live here," he said.

Bullshit, 100% bullshit. He had fallen in love with Discogirl, or so it seemed, and life as he once knew it had spiraled out of control. While she was taking care of her sick mother, he was running around with other working girls, doing lunch, taking them shopping, buying them a trinket here or there, and of course, having sex with them. By his own admission, he had four or five regular sluts on the side. But Discogirl had some unseen power over him. She was his kryptonite.

Discogirl must have sensed the ride on the gravy train was slowing, so she issued a proactive ultimatum; allow her to continue whoring (even though she was not a whore) or give her $1000 a month.

Fearful of losing his new love, he agreed to pay.

"I felt sorry for her," he said. "Her mother really is sick. I'm not sure what's

wrong with her but she can't move. She just lies in bed all day."

"Couldn't she work in an office or at a hotel?" I asked.

"Even if she got a job, it wouldn't be enough to cover her expenses," he said. "And her mother has no one to take care of her. That's why she takes care of her. I can't let her go back to work at the disco."

"She needs help, so now you're Captain Save-A-Ho? You're her white knight in shining armor? Stop being a sucker!"

Silence.

It took time to find what had transpired, but eventually I got the whole story.

They began living together, and began traveling through Southeast Asia, taking trips to Cambodia, Singapore, Indonesia, Hong Kong, Macau and Vietnam. He made a ridiculous attempt at explaining that the only reason why he went to these places was to search for products to export, but he knew that I knew what was really going on.

"I guess the mother's feeling better?" I asked.

"Her older sister is staying with her now."

"I thought she had no one to take care of her?"

They Call Me Farang

Terry put the sister on the payroll, to the tune of $500 a month. She made half this at her previous job.

Terry and Discogirl went everywhere together, always staying in four or five-star hotels and everywhere they went, he bought her a gift or souvenir. Of course, she needed, as opposed to wanted, new clothes for their trips. She had found her Moby Dick, her great white whale, and she was using him for everything she could get. It wasn't enough just to travel and stay in upscale hotels; she had to have new clothes. Having fun and living life on his terms, his savings dwindled, the dream of starting an export business thrown aside like a used snot rag.

After their trip to Macau, her sugar daddy coughed up 400,000 baht to rebuild her grandparent's house. Upon returning from Vietnam, their final trip together, she asked Terry to pay off the family Isuzu pickup truck. Unwilling to see the truth and mistaking lust and desire for love, he handed over 200,000 baht.

Down and down his account balance went, plummeting all the way down to $10,000 before he realized just how far he had sunk. A few weeks after paying off the pickup truck, she thrust her hand out again, this time asking for $1000 on top of her monthly stipend. For the first time, he turned her down.

"No money to give, sorry honey."

Right on cue, she bailed out. Just like that, true love fell by the wayside, she stopped coming around and he never saw or heard from Discogirl again. The love affair was over.

Ninety-thousand dollars — blown — gone forever, exchanged for sex, companionship and memories. Fortunately, he still had enough left to get back on his feet in the US. After pissing away a huge sum of money, some might think that he was an idiot. Maybe so, but he had one helluva time in the process.

Two months after leaving Bangkok, he called me. Within days of returning home, Terry scored a job earning more money than he made before he came to Bangkok.

The weekend after landing the job, he went out to a club to celebrate his new job with several of his friends. Shortly after arriving at the club, he spotted a longhaired Vietnamese girl with a body that forced him to muster up the courage to walk over and strike up a conversation with her. He got her number and several days later, they went out on their first date. Within a month, they were boyfriend and girlfriend and Thailand was a distant memory.

"I might come back for a visit when I get my vacation time," he said. "But I like my job and my new girlfriend is hot. I'll probably never live in Thailand. It's not for me."

"Never say never," I said.

This was my last conversation with Terry. Apparently he found enough of Asia in the US to keep him happy.

Scott Mallon
The Texan

"Texas is neither southern nor western. Texas is Texas."
William Blakley, U.S. Senator

***

When I first arrived in Thailand, I entered the country without a visa, staying for 30 days and then paying immigration to extend my stay for another 15 days. Once the fifteen-day extension expired, I left the country to start the process all over again. The majority of the time, I took a bus to the border, crossed into Cambodia, and then turned right back around and re-entered Thailand.

After a few visa runs, I smartened up, flew to Cambodia, and procured a one-year, multiple-entry tourist visa. Back in the late 90's it was much easier to get this type of visa and I used this to my advantage. With a one-year, multiple-entry tourist visa, I could stay in the country for two months, get a one-month extension, go out of the country, and within minutes turn right back around and stay for another three months. A day or two before the visa expired, I would fly out of the country and apply for another one-year, multiple-entry visa. Once my visa ran out though, my funds were running low and I had to figure out a cost effective way to remain in the country. Traveling outside of Thailand and staying a couple of nights in a different country is costly, even when staying on the cheap. The monthly payments from the sale of my business had stopped and I was desperate to cut costs, so I decided to forego getting another tourist visa. Instead, I would cross the border, obtain the necessary exit stamp from Thailand, cross into Cambodia, immediately turn around, then re-enter Thailand on a 30-day, visa exemption.

A border run would provide 45 more days in Thailand and my hope was that this would be sufficient time to come up with the funds to procure another one-year, multiple-entry visa.

I took a bus to Aranyaprathet and then crossed over into Poi Pet in Cambodia. Cambodian immigration officials stamped me into their country, stamped me out ten minutes later, and before I knew it, I was back in Aranyaprathet.

The bus back to Bangkok left in an hour, so I decided to grab a bite to eat. I walked over to a little dive of a restaurant across the street from the station, sat down, and placed my order.

The restaurant was similar to restaurants found everywhere in Thailand; cheap metal table, red and blue plastic chairs. A framed picture of the King of Thailand and a poster promoting Nescafe coffee graced the grimy wall. A grey-haired old man, the only other customer, sat in the corner reading the Bangkok Post.

A few seconds later, as I began to eat my soup, I heard his paper rustling and then the sound of his voice.

"You come here to get your visa?" he asked.

His drawl was thick and his voice had a twangy sound I had not heard in several years.

"Yep," I said.

"Me too," said the old man.

"Where ya from?"

"Miami," I said.

Each time I began to eat, he spoke.

"I'm from Waco."

Tall and lean, his name was Walter. In the course of our conversation, I learned that before retiring eight years ago, he had worked in the oil fields, his wife Vivian passed away three years ago and he had a 50-year-old son named Melvin who worked as an accountant. He also loved the Dallas Cowboys; he made it a point to explain how he loved the old Cowboys, the ones coached by Tom Landry when Roger Staubach was quarterback. The new Cowboys were "nothing but a bunch of overpaid drug addicts and perverts." Doctors had recently diagnosed Walter with diabetes.

With his weathered skin, long-sleeved western style shirt, Levis, and well-worn belt with a huge horse buckle and dirty cowboy boots, Walter was the spitting image of a cowboy. He topped off his look with a shabby, gray cowboy hat that probably hadn't been off his head in years.

"How long have you been here?" I asked.

"I moved here six months ago," he said. "How 'bout you?"

"Going on three years."

I went back to my noodles and sat in silence.

He fumbled with his newspaper, pushed away from the table, stood up, and walked slowly over to my table.

"Can I have my bill, please?" he said, smiling at the waitress.

I noded.

"Me too."

We said our goodbyes to the waitress and walked to the front of the restaurant.

"I like this place," he said. "But I sure have a hard time understanding everything!"

"Yea, I know what you mean."

We walked slowly towards the bus station.

"Do you speak any Thai?" I asked.

"Nooooo… their language is too foreign for me. About all I can say is *sa-wa-dee-khup*.

I chuckled involuntarily.

"Whaddya think about the women?" he asked.

"I try not to think about 'em too much," I said. "We'll never understand women, right? But here, forget about it. It's like pissin' in the wind."

We continued our conversation and boarded our bus. We took off for Bangkok and settled in. I was hoping to get a little shut-eye, but Walter wanted to talk.

"I met this old gal a couple of months ago," he said. "Right purty and sweet as they come. Thai women are so sweet."

They're all sweet in the beginning, I thought.

"Really? Where did you meet her?" I asked, ignoring his last comment and my internal dialogue.

Knowing Thai women and his inability to communicate, I was reluctant to believe he was able to land anything other than a bargirl.

"Well, I'll tell ya. On one of my visa runs, I went to Trat. On my way back, I stopped off in a little restaurant, kinda like this one."

At least he didn't fall for a bar girl covered in tattoos and slathered in gold.

"I had some noodle dish. It was so good I told the waitress to give my compliments to the chef."

This was getting interesting.

"She walked back through a set of doors and a few seconds later brought out this ole gal and tells me, 'This is cook.'"

"Like I told you, she was real purty, cute as a button," he said, emphasizing the word purty.

The old man was pure Americana.

"So you hooked up with her?" I asked, wanting to cut to the chase.

"She just stood there smiling," he said. "I didn't know what to think."

"Thais smile," I said. "Sometimes they smile because they're not sure what to do or say."

"Well, this girl didn't speak any English but I wrote down my name and address on a piece of paper, and the waitress told her what I said."

"What did you say?"

"I told her that if she ever came to Bangkok, she should give me a call."

"Uh huh… And did she?"

"She did more than that!" he said, laughing loudly. "She showed up on my doorstep."

"No!"

"Yes sir, she sure enough did. She's been staying with me for the last month."

"But you don't speak Thai and she doesn't speak

English, right? How's that work?"

He burst out in laughter.

"She don't speak English," he said, smacking the palm of his hand on his thigh. "But that don't stop her from talkin'!"

The old man was clearly at a loss for what to do.

"She's always a cookin' and a cleanin' or doing something around the house. She's a hard little worker," he said.

"How old is she?" I asked.

"Twenty-one."

He turned and looked at me.

"She talks to me all the time but I don't understand a word she says."

"Does she understand anything you say?"

"I don't know, but she never stops flappin' her gums," he said.

"You're sleeping with her though, right? I mean, can you still...?"

"Yes, sir."

"And?"

"We have our fun but I'm an old man. She's always a rarin' to go and can't get enough. She plum tuckers me out!"

By now, I was starting to like the old codger. While troubled by his predicament, at least he was having fun.

"Anytime we get in the taxi, she's always yappin' with the driver."

"She's probably dying to talk to someone," I said. "Can you blame her?"

"I didn't think she'd show up on-ma-doorstep though!"

"You could always give her the boot. It's only been a few weeks, shouldn't be too hard."

"That might be a little difficult," he said, scratching his head. "We got married earlier this week."

"Noooooo…. you didn't. You're fuckin' with me. You didn't really marry this girl, did you?"

"Yes sir, I sure enough did. She told me this is what they do here."

Initially, I thought a bucking bronc had kicked him upside his head and he was nuts. After all, the old coot had gone and married a girl he could barely communicate with, had little in common with, and who was young enough to be his granddaughter.

"You better learn to speak Thai," I said, still in shock. "Get her to an English school too."

"She's trying to teach me," he said. "But I don't think I'm a very good student. Their language is confusing."

By the time we reached Bangkok I realized while this was an irregular union by most standards, what he wanted most was a companion. He was lonely and this marriage was his adventure, probably the last of his life. With his wife gone and the majority of his friends retired or dead, he had moved to Thailand. Then he met a young woman who gave him something to live for; she had him feeling like a teenager again. Illogical, perhaps, but who could blame him?

The bus reached Bangkok just before midnight, we bid each other farewell and went our separate ways. I never saw the Texan again.

The Art of Nose Picking

"Love is like a booger. You keep picking at it until you get it, then wonder what to do with it."

Oscar Wilde, Irish Writer and Poet

***

The human nose is a logistical nightmare. Normally, people go through life without giving their nostrils much thought, except perhaps when full of gunk and their finger is in it knuckle deep. Unlike the lowly anus, hidden neatly from view, the nose ports are wide open for all to see. If someone accidentally leaves a dingle berry behind, it goes unseen. If they overlook their schnozzle and forget to pay attention, they could unknowingly walk all over town with a gelatinous, multi-colored blob dangling from their proboscis.

If you think about it, human bodies are disgusting in more than one way. Snot, boogers, flaky skin, ass sweat, ball sweat, bloody vaginas, gorilla-like backs, stinky feet, noxious gas from the ass, and other delightfully funky odors coming from who knows where are just a few of the things we attempt to dismiss or disguise. Some do a better job than others caring for their personal hygiene.

When it comes to people wiping their snot on money and then handing it to me, I feel the need to speak up. We have all sorts of funkiness going on inside and outside our bodies and unless you were born with a severe abnormality, we all have the same functional, yet nasty orifices.

Despite what people want to believe, we are animals, masses of flesh attempting to disguise reality. We scrub our bodies with soap and attempt to mask our natural scent with cologne and perfume. We like to think we are intelligent beings, civilized, better and smarter than all the other animals on the planet. Yet, for better or worse, we are all still animals.

All of us have issues with our bodies, which at some point in our lives materialize. There is nothing beautiful or cute about the goo residing in a person's nasal cavity and whether rich and famous or poor as a church mouse, there are no exceptions. Nasal waste graces the noses of Presidents, Prime Ministers, Kings, Queens, Princes and Princesses, and yes, even super models.

Ever sit in a food court, ogling a gorgeous girl with a body to die for as she unabashedly begins digging for hidden treasure? In Southeast Asia, it is quite common to see people picking their nose. There are those who take a sneaky, casual swipe or furtive dig and then there are those who take their nose picking as seriously as any gold miner does. These people think nothing of shamelessly engaging in hard-core pick-age no matter their location or situation.

Picking boogers is unhygienic and revolting. Just like shitting, nose picking is a matter best done in private. If someone actually sees the act of picking, this is too public. The art of nose picking is a private matter best done behind closed doors.

Compounding the nose picking nastiness, some Asian cultures rarely use toilet paper. If used, it is only to pat dry one's nether regions. Thais do not use corncobs, newspaper or leaves; they use water, and quite often, their hand. Using water to clean your rear is much cleaner and more pleasurable than using toilet paper, however; toilet paper in Thailand either falls apart in your hand or is like sandpaper. Thai bathrooms normally use a water hose, or bum gun, conveniently positioned within reach of the toilet. You spray into the crack, wash away the egesta, and go on your merry way. Presto! Absolute magic. No fuss, no muss, no itchiness, no skid marks in the underwear, nada!

Some Thai bathrooms have a large tank of water with a small, plastic bowl close by. You fill the bowl; pour the water down your backside, and the result is the same as with using the bum gun. Using the non-eating hand to wipe away the leftovers is the preferred method, and most people have the sense to wash their hands after defecating. How can you be sure though? Water washes away what is visible to the naked eye but only hot water can wash away any unseen fecal bacteria.

Have you ever seen a man with a long pinky fingernail? Have you ever considered its function? Without a doubt, the long pinky fingernail is part of the Asian nose picking process. Is it also part of the ass wiping process?

Nose picking in Asia is an art form, albeit a dreadful one.

Unfortunately, on more than one occasion I have had the misfortune of seeing a taxi driver or merchant in Chinatown ramming their pinky fingernail up their nose as if scraping the inside of a coke vial.

Does every cashier, sales clerk, taxi driver, delivery

person or other person we come into contact with in the course of our daily lives take the time to wash their hands? Do they use soap, hot water or handy wipes? Doubtful.

This means besides the person picking their nose, they might also have a layer of shitty bacteria ready to take over your body like an alien life form.

They wipe their rear, do a half-ass job (excuse the pun) of washing their hands, and then yank away at any foreign objects impeding their airways.

One taxi driver happily tugged away at a boulder-sized chunk of dried mucus while simultaneously asking about my taste in Thai women.

"You like big ass? Young girl? Massage?"

"I'm married," I say, coughing loudly as if to say, *'Hey, stop that, ya nasty bastard!'*

Rarely do I actually say anything though, instead praying that the traumatic experience ends quickly. I will turn my head away from the formalities and then cough and twitch like some poor fellow with Tourette's syndrome.

"You okay mistah?"

"No, I'm scarred for life," I think. *"Don't even look at me, ya nasty bastard! I'll put your money on the seat."*

"No problem!" I say, grimacing.

The driver hands me my change, of course, with a smile. I, however, am unable to muster a smile. He is probably wondering why I am so unhappy. Millions of people take their change blissfully unaware of the abominable transgressions transpiring every second of every day. After witnessing numerous Asians practicing the art of nose picking over dinner, in restrooms, walking down the street, and while in the midst of a heated discussion, I now comprehend why people become Germaphobes. I also have a better idea of why people engage in obsessive-compulsive hand washing.

As the cab rolls away, I glance inside making certain I have not left anything behind. After losing several phones and important documents, this has become habit. Out of the corner of my eye, I notice the driver's left hand back in action. Pick, pick, inspect, pick, pick, inspect. My brain further scarred, it dawns on me; I need to find a place to wash my hands.

Scott Mallon
Noise Pollution

"Nowadays most men lead lives of noisy desperation."
James Thurber, American cartoonist, journalist, author, playwright

***

The sky is blue and free of clouds, waves lapping the shoreline, softly, as if to avoid disrupting my sleep. Birds chirp and tweet to announce the start of the day, the whisper of the wind gently flowing through the air. Peace, at last, peace at last. Slowly, ever so slowly, I emerge from the darkness of sleep and re-enter the world of the living. It is an exceptional day, one I rarely experience, for when Mother Nature awakens me, she does so gently and I wake as I should, mellow and well rested.

In a split second though, a dreadful noise shocks me out of my comfortable bed in the bungalow, fifty feet from the water's edge. This is no nightmare though, this is reality, the land of noise, made by humans for humans. The whine of a saw growls in the distance, softly at first, then growing in ferocity as it tears through a slab of wood. In seconds, I am fully awake, an unwilling participant in the world over which I have no control, and at this moment, I wish I were sleeping in a cave. I am neither a deep sleeper nor a person who sleeps easily, but once awake, I am unable to return to dreamland. It is 6 AM.

The days leading up to my departure for the bungalow

on the beach in the South were filled with too much noise, too much motion, too much everything. Finally, with the chaos of Bangkok life grating on my nerves, I decided to get away. What I need is a change of scenery, an escape from the world, an odyssey into a self-enclosed bubble where calm takes precedence.

This time around, I scour the internet, carefully researching where I can find the last bastion of peace in Thailand. I come up with Koh Phayam. Situated off the coast of Ranong province, the island looks to be the peaceful getaway I so desperately need, a place to settle my thoughts and regroup, a place free of man-made sounds.

So early one evening, I hopped on a southbound bus towards my destination. I put on my headphones, turned on the soothing sounds of the ocean, and sleep for the majority of the nine-hour journey. By the time I arrived at the Ranong terminal, I was relaxed and in my own world. Mission accomplished, at least temporarily.

When the bus door opened, a toothless old man was there to greet the passengers one by one.

"Hello, hello, you go pier? Go island?" he said. "80 baht."

"Okay," I said. "No problem, let's go."

A total of six men and one woman jumped into the back of his pick-up truck. None of them spoke Thai so when I accepted the 80 baht fare, they did as well. A short drive later, we arrived in a pitch-black parking lot in front of the pier.

Ten minutes later, a short, squat woman with a huge smile and even larger ears walked through the crowd and up to one of the shop houses.

"Coffee? Anybody want coffee? Something to eat?" she asked, with a decidedly British accent.

"I'll take some coffee," I said. "Can you make an American breakfast?

"Yes, no problem."

Fifteen minutes later, another truckload of travelers pulled up, all backpackers. The parking lot was now full of 20 - 25 year olds, all milling about, eager to get to wherever it was they were going.

Just then, a woman on a motorcycle pulled up to the travel agency next door. She took off her helmet, unlocked the padlock and began turning on the lights inside her tiny office.

Moments later, she walked out front and gazed at the crowd.

"Where is everybody going?" she said, shouting to anyone willing to listen.

In unison, a dozen people in the group stepped forward, surrounding the woman.

"Koh Phayam," one of them said.

"Me too."

"Me too."

My spirits sank like the Titanic. If all these people were going to Koh Phayam, the island would be much less peaceful than I anticipated.

I ate my overpriced, poor excuse of an American breakfast and sipped my equally overpriced, instant coffee.

"Where are you going," asked Klaus, a sixty-something German who had been walking in circles for the past twenty minutes.

"Well, I was going to Koh Phayam… it looks like it's not as quiet as I thought, though."

"Ohhhhhh, Koh Phayam is not quiet," he said. "If you want quiet, Koh Chang is much better."

It turned out my hunch was right.

"Is that where you're going?" I asked.

"Yes. I come here every year and SCUBA dive. If you want a quiet place to go, Koh Phayam is not for you. There are many backpackers, bars, loud music… ahhhh, Koh Chang is much better for me."

Now finished with the backpackers, the woman from the travel agency walked towards me.

"Where are you going sir?

"Koh Chang. I want to go to Koh Chang."

"Three-hundred fifty baht," said the woman.

Three-hundred fifty baht, a small price to pay for transportation to a quiet island.

"The boat leaves at 8 AM."

There was nothing left to do but sit and wait.

In today's world, humans have become accustomed to life's daily cacophonies; save for going into the jungle, quiet and solitude in Thailand are on the verge of extinction. I notice excessive noise though, a curse to my ears and scrambled senses. Noise disturbs, disrupts, distracts, and discombobulates like a hammer to the head, and as I have grown older, my quest for peace and quiet has increased. Radios blare, televisions hiss, bells ring, motorcycle engines roar, children scream and cry, computers buzz, air-conditioners hum and old women cackle; ubiquitous, ceaseless, unrelenting, noise.

One of the rudest, most despicable noise-emitting products ever invented, is the alarm clock. Oh, how I despise the alarm clock and all it represents. Instead of allowing a person to wake naturally, the alarm clock shakes, stirs, and frightens the unconscious into consciousness. A dreadful way to start any day.

Noise defined is the non-harmonious or discordant group of sounds. Tranquility is more elusive every second, and those yearning for it now must hunt for it like a wild animal. Perhaps my aversion to noise is a sign of old age, or perhaps, I am hypersensitive. I think not though, for I still enjoy listening to loud music, usually rock and roll, and my wife is constantly reminding me to turn down the volume.

"The neighbors are complaining, and they say they can hear your music all the way down the street! Are you deaf?"

I admit, I sometimes create my own noise pollution, but most of the time, especially when the wife is around, I wear headphones and keep the pollution to myself. When I am the source of the noise, I embarrass her; when others make noise, she tells me to ignore it. Of course, I tell her to shut up. The last thing I want to hear is her grumbling.

What is it with Thais and noise? They seem to have an unlimited tolerance to excessive decibels and are oblivious or apathetic about the noise around them.

In Thai department stores, malls, and grocery stores, it is common practice for two or three good-looking young ladies, or *Pretties*, to take up a strategic position in an area with the highest number of shoppers, and then launch into a skit designed to get shoppers to buy their products.

"Today only, all Acme whitening products for women are 25% off!" says Pretty Girl #1, beaming with youthful enthusiasm. "Acme's magical products guarantee you'll look more white and even more beautiful!"

"Really? What do these products do?" asks Pretty Girl #2, jumping up and down like a giddy school girl. "Tell me more!"

Please, don't. I don't want to know more, I want to know less. More importantly, I want to hear less. And by the looks of the faces on the people in the vicinity, they want to hear less, too, only they are too timid to speak. Instead they nod and grin and walk away as quickly as they can. Whitening creams are the snake oil of the modern times and anytime I hear these irritating shills, I always feel the urge to walk over and say, "Will you please shut the fuck up? Nobody wants to hear you!"

Politely, of course. In keeping with societal norms, though, I walk by, give them my best phony smile, and keep my thoughts of bending them over to myself. Try selling this junk in America and see how long they last.

Sales people are bad enough, always hovering, grinning, and circling like sharks preparing for the kill, but giving them megaphones only further violates the air waves. It's downright criminal.

To make matters worse, they lie like used car salesmen, say anything necessary to make the sale.

"It's so beautiful."

I don't think so.

"It's inexpensive."

Then you buy it for me.

"Very good quality."

Made in China, this thing is a piece of shit that's going to fall apart in under a month.

"The owner only drove the car once."

Right, and a little old lady from Pasadena used to own it.

Always about the sale, the money, and using whatever phoniness necessary to reel in the cash. The sale, the sale, the sale, get that money, even if it means cramming their noise down your throat.

Noise is all consuming, no matter the hour. Early morning in my village sounds like a gathering place for a gaggle of cackling, pre-menstrual hens.

"I think it's going to rain today!"

"No, I don't think so. The rain will not reach us."

"Well, I hope it doesn't rain. I need to make money today."

"How's your daughter?"

"Oh, she is very good! Did I tell you she's getting married?"

"Really? When? Who is she marrying? I hope you get a lot of money!"

"She is marrying a foreigner. I only saw him on the computer but I don't like him, but he will give us money so I am nice to him."

Every morning, every day, my female neighbors yap amongst themselves. More useless conversation — more noise pollution.

They Call Me Farang

Around the same time, every morning, every day, a pick-up truck will drive by. This is no ordinary pick-up truck though, this is a pick-up truck with a huge megaphone on top of it, one of several that drives through the village every morning, every day and without fail.

"Today only, get our delicious Pad Thai for only 30 baht!"

Wonderful, but it's not fresh. Maybe you should shut up.

"Get your fresh vegetables, fresh fruit. Buy now!"

If I want vegetables, there is a fresh market within walking distance. Keep the noise down — before I shoot you!

"Tomorrow afternoon at 3:30, go see the Muay Thai show next to Wat Theep Lila. World champions! It's free! Don't miss it!"

If I want to watch Muay Thai, I'll turn on the TV or go to Lumpini or Rajdamnern Stadium. I don't need you to wake me up to get me to watch it! You wanna box right now? We'll put on our own show for the village.

A flyer in my mailbox would work just as well and would be far less irritating. Obviously these truck drivers get some sick satisfaction from waking people in the neighborhood.

More noise pollution.

With the saw shredding my ear drums and now unable to sleep, I climb out of bed, and step to the window. Off in the distance stand two men. One with a circular saw in his hand, another, a rotund fellow in his sixties, who looks to be giving instructions. They are standing next to a half-constructed bungalow, one of a dozen bungalows spread out on the property. Had I been completely awake, I might have walked over and gave each of them a solid shot to the nose. Instead, I pour hot water into my coffee cup, give the liquid a quick stir, then walk out onto the front porch where I sit down.

Don't they know people are trying to sleep? Don't they know why we are here? Why on earth would someone start sawing and hammering at 6 AM?

I sip my coffee and for a brief moment, contemplate walking over to the main building on the complex to have a chat with the owner. However, laziness prevails and I kept my ass planted in the chair, feet propped up on the porch railing. The main building is a ten-minute walk from my bungalow and I have no desire to move. The fan and light above my head stops working. The electricity on the island is only switched on four to six hours per day and someone has shut it off. For now, silence returns.

An hour later, after a hearty breakfast, I go out for a swim, then take a leisurely stroll down the beach. An elderly woman, in her seventies, tan and sinewy, walks out from a house behind a group of trees. We exchange smiles and I continue my walk. Alone in my thoughts, I walk for an hour before turning around to return to my bungalow. The same woman is sitting in the sand, meditating in a half-lotus position. I walk past her, thinking she might open her eyes and smile or say hello, but she is in the zone and does not flinch. Looks like she's managed to find her peace.

Then it hits me. Erect an impenetrable, invisible wall around me and block out the unwanted noise; after all, peace comes from within.

Peace comes from within… Ohhhhhmmmmmm.

Peace comes from within… Ohhhhhmmmmmm.

Peace comes from within… Ohhhhhmmmmmm.

I return home to Bangkok and the noise returns, slowly at first, eventually becoming overwhelming again. I try using the wall and remind myself peace comes from within.

Peace comes from within… Ohhhhhmmmmmm.

It doesn't work. The noise on the outside crashes through my wall and into the middle of my inner peace. Peace comes from within, but when you're sitting on a quiet beach or in the middle of the forest, it's much easier to find than in the middle of a busy city.

Scott Mallon
The Faucet

"Love is like a faucet (it turns off and on)."
Billie Holiday, American jazz singer

***

Dink — dink — dink — dink.

The faucet in my kitchen was leaking water and stopping it was growing more difficult. The drips first came in thirty-second intervals; then faster, until the water became a steady stream of drips. When sitting on the sofa, my favorite spot to watch TV, I could hear the sound of the water hitting the steel sink. As the frequency of the drops increased, so did my frustration.

Each time I used the faucet there was a fierce battle to stop the drip. Once I stopped the leak, I would declare myself the victor. I thought I conquered my foe. Gone was the noise, no longer would it torture my nerves. Or so I thought. Like cancer, the noise would return, tiny droplets crashing down upon the sink like boulders.

This interminable sound, why does it torment me so?

I walked upstairs and closed the door. At last, silence!

When the night was as silent as death and my wife and children slept in peace, the sound returned again. Teasing at first, soft and distant, muffled, increasing in volume and clarity, taunting me.

Dink — dink — dink — dink.

Is there no peace? Will it ever stop?

As hard as I tried, the dripping sound always returned, faster, stronger, LOUDER! Peace was proving to be ephemeral.

The next morning, I walked down the street to my landlord's house and asked if she would send her handyman around. Every other time we needed him, he showed up within an hour or two, problem solved. Alas, it was the Thai New Year and he was on a hard whiskey ride and would not return for several days. I would either need to fix the leaky faucet myself or wait for the landlord's backup handyman. He too was on the whiskey.

The sound grew sharper and more distinct. I could take it no longer. I cursed the sink, the faucet, the house and everything inside it. Then I walked outside to the front of my house, sat on a chair, propped my feet up and began contemplating the meaning of life.

April is a stupid time for a new year. Thailand should have their new year in January, like most other countries in the world.

Three minutes into my deep thought, I decided that instead of enduring further agony, I would send the wife out to buy a new faucet.

"Go buy a faucet and I'll fix it," I said. "This dripping sound is driving me nuts."

"I'm not going out anywhere today," she said. "It's too hot and I have things to do."

"Noooo, this is a serious problem, I want this thing fixed!"

"Go get it yourself!" she said.

"C'mon, you know my hip is hurtin' honey. I can hardly

walk!"

"Yea, right," she said, giving me the evil eye.

"Just go out, buy what we need, and I'll do the rest, promise!" I said, crossing my fingers.

An hour later, she returned with the faucet and a steel braided hose meant to connect the faucet to the fitting jutting out from the wall. Without hesitation, she popped down under the sink and examined the dilemma. The wife is quite the handy woman, capable of fixing just about anything with or without tools. Although I too am capable of fixing anything that might need fixing, in my house I am the lion, the head of the pride, and thus, lazy.

When our roof began leaking in my office during the rainy season, the wife took it upon herself to climb the tree next to our house to get up to the roof. She leaped from the tree to the roof, applied some magical concoction and seconds later, no more leak. Afterward, I got questions.

"Don't you think this is the man's job?"

"Why did I have to go up there?"

"I'm a woman, why am I the only one fixing everything around here?"

"Equal rights," I said, chuckling.

Had she informed me she was going up on the roof to do a repair, I would have handled the matter my way, I would have paid someone to patch the hole. For weeks after repairing the roof, she felt the need to remind me not to shirk my household duties. As head lion and the man of the house, I was under the impression I had none.

She climbed out from under the sink, mumbling under her breath as she walked away. I seized the opportunity and opened the cabinet beneath the sink to look for the shutoff valve. No luck. I followed the hose under the sink out through the side of the cabinet and lo and behold, right next to our refrigerator and up against the wall, was a goo-covered, red plastic shutoff valve. The thick gunk had dried and locked the valve in place. Not wanting to break the valve and cause a flood, I sent the wife out front to shut off the main water valve. Using my trusty Swiss Army knife, I sliced through the crud and peeled it away until the valve moved. I cut through the thick, plastic packaging, removed the faucet and placed it on the counter.

Mrs. Fix-it came back with her rusty needle-nose pliers and a determined look on her face.

"Move," she said.

Before I could say a word, she grabbed the faucet and was pushing it up through the hole in the counter. I took hold of the faucet and attempted to pull it into place. It didn't fit. Without first removing the nut, the faucet would never fit.

I heard a grunt and my wife rose from the classic, under-the-sink plumber's position and ripped the faucet out of my hands. Holding it in two hands like a knife, she attempted to place it through the hole in the top of the counter, noticed the improper fit and slapped on a rubber washer. She began stabbing the faucet through the hole in the counter in a manner every bit as sinister as Norman Bates. The counter bounced up and down like an earthquake was rolling through our kitchen.

Patience never was one of her virtues.

"Hey! What are you doing?" I said, as I snatched the

faucet from her.

"You have to take the nut off, put the faucet through the hole, then tighten the nut on the faucet from underneath the sink."

Sneer. Sigh. Snicker.

She took off the rubber washer from the old faucet and put it on the new one. If one washer is not enough, two must be better. Wrong.

"You don't need that second washer!" I said. "There's one on it already! Where's the crescent wrench?"

"What's that?"

"The big silver wrench, where is it? That's what we need," I said, shaking my head in disbelief. "Always make sure you have the right tools for the job," I said, quoting my father. "I know we have one around here somewhere."

She held up her needle-nose pliers as if she already had what she needed. These crappy little pliers were her go-to tool in every fix-it situation. They were her hammer, wrench, pliers, vice grips, and screwdriver all rolled up in one.

Never one to admit defeat, she took off the nut, dropped back down under the sink, then turned it on the threads of the faucet. My job was to hold the faucet in place to prevent it from turning.

"Why don't you let me do that?" I said. "If you go and find the crescent wrench it'll only take me a second to fix this."

"Your leg is bad, remember?" she said, rolling her eyes. "I can do it."

Smart-ass. Her insistence and determination were

normally admirable traits, but at this moment, they were traits that made me want to put my foot up her ass.

"Okay," I said, sarcastically. "You let me know if you need any help. I would have been done by now."

She required no help. A few seconds later, the new faucet was in, with no leaks.

"If it was so easy to fix, why didn't you do it yourself?" she said.

I knew better than to prolong the conversation. I walked outside, sat in my chair, put my feet up, and did nothing for the rest of the day, like a lion king. Days later, the faucet was still working. And I was still doing nothing.

Scott Mallon
When You Gotta Go, Go!

"Never kick a fresh turd on a hot day."
　　Harry S. Truman, 33rd President of the United States

***

I was desperate to get out of Bangkok. If I don't get away every couple of months to recharge my batteries, I get irritable and combative. Living in a big city will do this to a person.

I decided to leave for Kanchanaburi on Thursday morning. I would stay for three or four days, maybe longer, depending on how I felt. The city is the home of the *Bridge Over the River Kwai*, made famous in the movie and novel of the same name. The bridge is the start of the Death Railway that leads to Myanmar (formerly Burma). Constructed during World War II by POWs and slave laborers, thousands lost their lives in the process.

The area is now home to a thriving backpacker community and is a huge tourist destination. This happens all over the world; kill thousands, even millions of people, then make the scene of the atrocity a tourist attraction.

My funds were limited so I checked in to The Jolly Frog, a cheap guesthouse popular with the backpacker crowd. I normally stay at higher end establishments but I promised my wife I would be frugal and would forego the four or five-star hotels. The finest room at The Jolly Frog, which isn't saying much, was only 290 baht ($9.50), so I splurged. The location was decent, just off the main road, and if you sat on one of the numerous lawn chairs or hammocks, the view of the river attractive. Not a bad deal, considering the price, and good enough for a night or two.

The rooms surround a large garden, which in turn provided a good view of the river. My room was old, the paint on the wall peeling, and an indistinguishable smell lingered throughout. The air-conditioner sounded like a jet engine but worked like a champ. This was important for just about everywhere in Southeast Asia, a good air-conditioner is mandatory; a weak air-conditioner is a deal breaker. The bed was soft, too soft, but the room served its purpose and my only concern was that the room was void of rats and roaches.

Every morning, I dined at the indoor-outdoor restaurant in the guesthouse, then walked around the town looking for good light and memorable photographs. I took breaks when I grew tired, ate when I was hungry and took my time getting to know Kanchanaburi. I was in no hurry.

After a long, uneventful day, I headed back towards the hotel. It was hot, as Thailand is ordinarily, and I was thirsty, so I stopped at a small, roadside shack selling drinks and snacks. The little drink kiosks are common throughout Thailand and come in handy in times of need.

As I walked towards the shop, an attractive girl turned and smiled.

"Hello, can I help you?" she asked, cheerfully.
"What do you have to drink?" I asked.

"Water, Coke, Sprite, Fanta orange, Fanta red, Fanta green, Thai tea with milk, Thai lemon tea, coffee, and cocoa. We have fruit juice and fruit shakes too: orange, pineapple, banana, and watermelon."

"I'll have a pineapple shake," I said.

"Would you like something to eat?" she asked. "I can make you Thai food."

"No, thank you, I'm not hungry." I said.

"Where do you come from?" she asked.

"America. What about you? Are you from Kanchanaburi?"

"Yes."

She pulled out a frozen pineapple, chopped it up, and slid over to the blender. I sat back, looked around, and looked back at her. Her skin was lighter than most and her body fresh and taut. Thai men were going nuts over her, no doubt.

"Your English is very good," I said. "Where did you learn?"

"I study English in school and there are many *farang* in Kanchanaburi," she said, as she handed me my shake. "I think my English is not so good. I need more practice."

"Thank you," I said, looking in her eyes. The cold pineapple went down well. "Your English is good, really."

She laughed. "No, I don't think so."

"How long you stay in Thailand? You speak Thai very well."

"About ten years."

"Oh, ten years. I think you have Thai wife."

I smiled and looked out towards the main road.

"You're my first customer."

"Really?"

"Yes, really," she said, as she walked over to the sink. "Today is the first day I am open."

Being the first customer of the day at a Thai business supposedly brings good luck. I can use all the luck I can get.

She moved away and wiped the counter clean.

My stomach grumbled and I suddenly felt nauseous. I thought nothing of it though, chalking it up to the heat and sweating. The grumbling continued growing louder though, until my lovely host turned and giggled.

"You want something to eat?" she asked. "I can make you something, no problem. And not expensive."

"No, no thank you, I'm okay." I wasn't hungry, I felt sick to my stomach.

Although my body had cooled down, my stomach had taken a turn for the worse.

"You should eat!" she said, shaking her head. "I am a good cook."

The growling continued for several minutes before I realized, *I needed to have a shit!* I had to get back to The Jolly Frog – fast.

"I need to go back to my hotel," I said. She had no idea that literally *I had to go.*

"So soon?" she said, looking disappointed. "Where are you going?"

"I have something I have to do. I'm sorry."

Struggling to remain calm, I handed her fifty baht, threw my bag over my shoulder, and stood up.

"Your change," she said.

"No, no, it's for you." I said, as I turned around. "Good

luck with your business, I'm sure you will do well!"

I smiled, then walked towards the main road as nonchalantly as possible.

"Please come back again, nice to meet you!" she said.

Without looking back, I threw my right arm up in the air and gave a half-hearted wave. My stomach was growling and hissing like a cat in heat. I had one objective, to make it back to the hotel before involuntarily purging my bowels. As soon as I reached the main drag, I released a long, gaseous fart. The fart provided a sliver of relief, but I knew I had to get to a toilet quick-like.

It was a ten-minute, straight shot to the guesthouse. The situation grew more pressing with every second but I was certain I could make it back and avoid an accident. Halfway back to the guesthouse though, painful stomach cramps brought me to my knees. I stopped on the side of the road and fought a life and death battle against the urge to purge. Sweat poured from every pore and my stomach lurched violently.

Whatever it was that had me in its grasp was powerful. I clenched my ass cheeks together, tightened my sphincter and walked as fast as possible. Every step was a battle and I looked like a speed walker with an iron rod jammed up his rear. I no longer cared how I looked though. I needed relief and needed it fast.

Moments later, I arrived at the hotel grounds. *Finally.*

Fumbling with my keys, I raced to my room. The door was in sight and I closed the distance. *Almost.* I grabbed the doorknob and jammed the key into the slot. Wrong key! I jumped up and down to stave off elimination.

Almost. Please!

I tried again, stuffed the key into the slot and turned.

I raced to the bathroom, shoved my pants and underwear to the floor, leaped to the toilet, then turned, took aim and let loose.

"Arrrggghhh."

Relief.

I sat back on to the toilet. In my haste, I did not turn the light on. The toilet seat and seat cover was down and I was sitting in my shit. My ass cheeks and the back of my legs were wet and a horrid; acrid smell blasted my nostrils. Instead of sitting down with a book as I normally did, I rushed the job. Now, I was paying for it.

I held my breath, stood up, walked over to the wall and turned on the light. There was shit splatter on the floor, the toilet, the wall, and all over my body. I spent the next thirty minutes cleaning the mess. The aroma of newly sprayed shit took on an ammonia smell that remains ingrained in my memory. Considering the torturous walk, the time spent cleaning was a small price to pay. I could have fouled myself in front of the girl at the drink stand and walked back to the Jolly Frog with shitty pants.

Once I completed the cleanup and showered, I walked across the street to a small pharmacy, bought a strip of Doxycycline, and downed two tablets. By the following afternoon, my stomach was less volatile and I was capable of taking a bus home.

When I arrived, I threw my backpack down to the floor and sank into the sofa.

"How was your trip honey?" asked my wife.

"Don't ask," I said.

It would be years before I told her what happened. Later, my son Alex had his own accident and I told him the story. Daddy taking a messy dump made him feel better. That's what Dad's are for, I guess.

If you shit all over yourself, all you can really do is shrug your shoulders. And clean up the mess.

Thai Bar Girls

"I believe that sex is one of the most beautiful, natural, wholesome things that money can buy."
Steve Martin, American Actor, Comedian, Musician

***

Before beginning my diatribe, let me state for the record I do understand the utilitarian properties of the Thai bar girl. Why, if it weren't for my wife-who I shall not preface with any adjective such as lovely, sweet, adorable, or kind-hearted (as so many seem to like to do when speaking of their Thai wife)-my own proclivity for ladies-for-hire would probably get the better of me. Yes, if it were not for the wife, and my general shortage of discretionary funds, I would live like a sheikh, and a harem I would have.

With ample funds, a different girl for each day of the month would be my bare minimum; Viagra and Cialis would rest in bowls strategically placed throughout the house like M and M's at a Van Halen concert. Moreover, nudity would be mandatory, and all of my girls would live on location, in their own bunkhouse. Of course, in addition to handling my sexual needs, they would double as my secretaries, cooks, maids, and personal assistants.

Scores of young men come to Thailand to sow their oats, hopping from bar to bar, drinking and screwing to the point of exhaustion, and having the time of their lives. For elderly men wanting to relive their halcyon days of youth,

Thailand is an ideal destination. Where else on earth can you find such a superfluity of seventy-year-old men walking hand in hand with teenyboppers young enough to be their granddaughters? Is it any wonder so many men want to live in the country?

There is nothing wrong with going to a bar, paying a few baht for companionship, and having your male needs satisfied. If women are willing to sell their bodies, and men are willing to buy them, why stand in the way of prosperity and sexual gratification? I am not here to debate the morals of prostitution. In Southeast Asia, prostitution is the norm. Sometimes hidden, often in your face, and the industry is a source of incredible revenue. For the time being at least, the world's oldest profession is here to stay.

Anyhow, I digress. Several years ago, I happened upon a documentary, *Love Me Long Time, Sex Tourism in Thailand.*

The movie is supposed to be a semi-cute tribute to those bar flies who fail to remember *The Golden Rule; Do Not Get Emotionally Involved With a Prostitute.* They become a Thai bar girl's umpteenth customer and then the hammer of love slams down upon them. Men, I implore you—wake up and crawl out of the fog. Hit the bars full force, have fun, play grab ass with the girls, have them show you the ways of Thailand but do not, under any circumstances fall in love and marry them!

The love interests of the men in the movie are the bottom of the barrel of Thai society and look like they too had been hit with a hammer. Smack dab in the face. Then again, the men were certainly no prize either.

They Call Me Farang

In all fairness to true documentary filmmakers like Ken Burns, Hugo Van Lawick, and Theodore Grouya, *Love Me Long Time, Sex Tourism in Thailand* closer resembles a home movie than documentary. Nevertheless, the depiction of just how screwed up men can be once they set foot in the Land of Smiles is dead on and painfully real. The documentary gives a glimpse into the warped minds of men hell-bent on giving up everything to live a life of debauchery, banging as many women as humanly possible, or at least as many as their girl of the moment allows.

Beauty is supposedly in the eye of the beholder, but if you are foolish enough to get involved with, or God forbid, marry a bar girl, at least make sure she's the sort of woman who makes others stare in awe of your manliness (or the ability to pay for it). If your girl oozes sexuality and her pulchritude is beyond reproach, at least people will chalk up your stupidity to man's inclination to think with the little head instead of the big one.

In one comical, yet sad sequence, a young man professes his love for his preferred bar girl. Later in the movie, he snivels about how a bank transfer from the UK failed to materialize and how the love of his life has now found another man. True love, yes, indeed.

To his credit, he acknowledges, "If my money comes tomorrow, she'll be back."

Another man continually states how special his girl is and tells how each month he provides a stipend so she can pay the rent. Apparently, he was not paying enough though because his girl continued to work in the bar and sleep with customers.

Most problems between foreigners and Thai bar girls stem from money, or the lack of it, and the inability to communicate properly and understand one other. Prostitutes work for one reason, to make money. Contrary to what the average punter may believe, the vast majority do not view themselves as the next *Pretty Woman.*

Money buys a place in line and rarely buys the love men desire. It is a bar girl's job to extract as much money as possible from their customer while at the same time making them feel like a million bucks. A good whore will get more money from her man than he wanted to give and leave him feeling handsome, sexy, special and manly. The constant never changes. Customer pays supplier, supplier provides the product. Done deal. With any luck, the man has his fun; the woman does her job, and both depart mutually satisfied with the transaction.

There will always be men claiming their former bar girl turned wife is exceptional. Men marrying prostitutes are either stupid, naïve, or know how to control them — with money. Those I have spoken with get irate when they hear me telling others to abstain from falling in love with bar girls. Tough shit. Without a doubt, there are good prostitutes out there. But to recommend a prostitute as a wife is life telling a gambler to bet his life savings on the lottery. Yes, there is a chance of winning, but the chance is slim to none.

Working girls may genuinely like and care for their client, and in some cases, one or both of those involved may develop an emotional and romantic connection. However, for most working girls, it is a job, no more, no less and far too many men who visit or reside in Thailand mistake kindness, attentiveness, sweet talk, and hot, passionate sex for love. Interactions with bar girls are a business transaction. The sooner men come to grips with this, the sooner they can face reality; falling madly in love with bar girls and making vain attempts to convert whores into housewives is a losing proposition.

Scott Mallon
One Last Fight

"Life is a story with many different endings."

Unknown

***

In 2010, I was working as a coordinator, manager, and trainer for Top Rated Boxing Promotions, a new company based in Bangkok made up of a small group of foreigners and Thais. After putting on several promotions in Thailand, the company attempted to crack the Singaporean market, promoting an event at the Suntec International Convention and Exhibition Centre. The show featured boxers from Australia, China, Indonesia, Guyana, Japan, Korea, Philippines, and Singapore. All six of our fighters won and although the event lost money, our primary goal was to get Resort's World Casino to co-promote a world title fight. We came close to succeeding only to have the deal unravel when the casino opted to put on a Mixed Martial Arts events instead of professional boxing.

Once our show was over, there were numerous loose ends to tie up before returning to Bangkok, so I remained in Singapore for an additional week. The work was minimal, the pay good and I had a penthouse suite at the Conrad Hotel overlooking the city. Boxing has always been a passion of mine and the company's future looked bright, so I was more than willing to stay behind and finish the job. During the day I worked, during the evening I went out on the town.

One of my favorite after-dinner venues was Orchard Towers, also known as *The Four Floors of Whores*. A large complex consisting of a hotel, offices, gift shops, and bars, Orchard Towers doubles as one of the main adult entertainment areas in Singapore. By day, the building looks every bit as reputable as any other building in Singapore; by night, it draws in men like a donkey with a hard-on tempts a Mexican whore. Our team often went there to relax and I knew the place well.

The night before returning to Bangkok, I decided to take one last trip to the Ipanema Bar. Located on the second floor, the bar was one of the more popular establishments in Orchard Towers, with live music, a dance floor, and a pool table. Weeks earlier, I talked the bar's manager into promoting our show in exchange for ten pairs of free tickets for his patrons.

Next door to Ipanema, under the same ownership, was the Bongo Bar. The Bongo Bar also had live music, but the reason I liked the place was the Coyote dancers, all of whom were from Thailand. Over the course of my time in Singapore, I got friendly with some of the girls, even putting a couple of them to work passing out fliers promoting our event.

The music was loud, making it difficult to hear, however, on this evening, there were few customers and the breaks between songs were longer than usual. During one of the lulls, I heard what sounded like men screaming at one another. Several of the dancers ran outside to watch from the walkway. I remained on my stool, sipping at my water. One of the girls ran back inside, plopped down on the stool next to me.

"Security is fighting with two Indian men," she said, giggling. "Boxing."

"That's nice," I said. "I'm tired, I'm going back to my hotel."

I paid the bill, walked out to the protective railing on the walkway, and looked down.

A pair of Indian men and two Singaporean bouncers stood face to face, screaming at one another. Seconds later, the Indians backed away from the bouncers, turned, then walked towards the exit, muttering expletives out the sides of their mouths. Excitement over — or so I thought.

I walked down the non-functioning escalator to the ground floor. As I reached the steps to the front entrance, two ladyboys walked towards me.

"Hello. What's your name?"

"My name's Joe, G.I. Joe," I said, grinning.

People often marvel at the beauty of ladyboys, but having seen thousands in Southeast Asia, I am of the opinion most look like men in drag. Why an unattractive man with the body of a linebacker would think he could pull off being an attractive woman is a mystery to me.

To each his own, I guess.

The thick, linebacker-type gave me the once-over.

"Tee-hee-hee!" he said, cackling. "You want lady?"

I paused for a moment before looking them both up and down.

"We give you good time," said the other, a tall, rail-thin thing with a pock marked face.

"I'm sorry, I like ladies," I said. "My wife would be angry if I went with you."

"I don't tell," said the beanpole. "Promise!"

"No, no. I only like women."

Then, the tone of the burly one changed, startling me.

"I am lady, you see!"

Before I could comprehend what was happening, it reached down, flipped the front its skirt back to reveal a bald patch of skin that looked exactly like a vagina. No panties, no hair, not a trace of a penis. Only a hairless slit.

Good job, doc, it sure looks like lady bits.

"I like real ladies. Sorry, you are not a real lady," I said.

A crowd was forming around us, the sounds of their laughter echoing through the night.

"I told you I am a lady!" one of them said, screaming. Cleary, it took offense to my comment.

They both stepped towards me, forcing me down the small set of stairs in front of the entrance to the foyer in front of the escalator. The heavyset one proceeded to take off one of its' high heels; our confrontation was about to get physical.

Anytime an angry ladyboy removes a shoe or belt, it's go time.

Big boy stepped within range and reared back to hit me with its shoe. As it did, I brought my left arm up to block the side of my face and launched a short, straight right at its jaw. The punch landed perfectly and it fell back and crumpled into the corner, out cold.

I spun left and turned to my second attacker. A pair of long nails dug into my scalp. Instinctively, I slid sideways, creating space to retaliate, then threw a quick one-two. The jab brought the hands up, a split second later, they dropped down to its' waist. The moment the hands began to fall, the right hand landed flush to the point of the jaw. My adversary was unconscious before hitting the ground.

Slightly stunned, I stood silent for a moment taking in the aftermath. I had surprised myself. Several people began clapping. I heard a voice behind me and turned to see the Mamasan from the Bongo Bar.

"You need to go," she said. "The police are coming."

This was all I needed to hear. I walked towards the back of the building. As I made my way for the door, the two bouncers who had been fighting with the Indians moments ago walked by me.

"You need to get out of here. The police are coming."

"I'm leaving," I said.

I walked towards the back of the building. As I closed in on the exit, I heard a shout. One of the two sleeping beauties had awakened with a hair out of place.

"I kill you motherfucker!" it said, screaming.

Perhaps I should have hit it harder.

Out of the corner of my eye, I could see it running towards me.

I looked out the exit and there, with its' door open like a gift from the heavens above, was a taxi. Several people were milling around at the taxi stand, but there was no queue. I ran towards the taxi and leaped on the back seat, quickly closing and locking the door.

"Conrad Hotel," I said, breathing quickly.

The taxi slowly began pulling away just as the princess

exited the building. Two feet away, it was impossible not to see me. Just like in a Starsky and Hutch episode, the beast jumped on the hood of the taxi, grabbing at the front window and hood, screaming.

"I will cut your dick off! I kill you!"

"Hey, what are you doing?" the driver said. He was old and frail and looked like he was about to have a heart attack.

"Drive," I said. "Go…go!"

He looked at me, then at the ladyboy, and pressed the accelerator.

The ladyboy hung on for the first fifty feet, our speed increasing as we approached the intersection. It fell off, bounced up off the asphalt road, rolled several times, then popped up and continued screaming. The stoplight changed from red to green and we sped away into the night. I had escaped unscathed.

Having the Singaporean police throw me in the clink was the last thing I wanted. The prospect of having my butt flesh split open like a watermelon with a cane was even less unappealing. My boss would bail me out, but he would be less than thrilled. He might laugh months later, but there would be hell to pay during the interim. My wife would probably divorce me. Years prior, after knocking out a Dane's teeth in a brawl at the Thermae Coffee Shop, she paid my bail and kept me out of jail. Afterwards, she made it a point to tell me not to expect her help ever again if I got into a fight. Never one to heed warnings, I had two more in the next year.

The driver turned to me, smiling.

"My friend, what happened?"

"That thing started a fight with me," I said, stretching the truth. "I finished it."

Blood oozed from the scratches on my forehead and for the first time since the incident, a twinge of pain set in. Aside from a couple of scratches and a bump or two, I was unscathed. I took out my handkerchief and dabbed at the blood. As soon as we reached the hotel, I went up to my room, showered and drifted off to sleep.

The next morning I flew back to Bangkok.

No time in a Singapore jail. I made it!

Weeks later, business required me to travel to Singapore once again. For whatever reason, as soon as I got a chance, I went back to the Bongo Bar.

"You fight good! Make them were very angry," said the Mamasan, laughing.

I said nothing. I wasn't sure what to say.

"Before you fight with them, they make problems with many foreigners. Now they stop."

"That's nice," I said, flatly.

My concern for the other patrons was nonexistent and the truth was that while I was defending myself, part of me wanted to see if I still had a little something left.

Only a few weeks earlier, I stood before the Singaporean press and proclaimed our company boxing's savior in Southeast Asia. I was ashamed — sort of — for I knew I could have smiled, said nothing, walked away and avoided conflict. I could have and should have — but I didn't.

Did I knock out two men or two women?

They Call Me Farang

Scott Mallon

Thai Woman vs. American Women

"Girls have an unfair advantage over men; if they can't get what they want by being smart, they can get it by being dumb."

Yul Brynner

***

A man once wrote me asking my opinion on how Thai women compare with American women. *"What are the Thai women like... are they like American women? I see a lot of American men finding wives there... how hard is it?"*

"It's as easy or difficult as you want it to be," I said, intentionally responding to his loaded question without giving him a concrete answer. "It also matters how comfortable you are being alone."

To answer means stereotyping not one, but two nationalities of women. No easy task, but my answer is an opinion and I am generalizing for the purpose of discussion.

Men and women have their share of differences, but both long for the best life possible; a close-knit family, good friends, a little love, a hug and a kiss now and then, passion, money, sex, children, grandchildren and a gadget or two. In short, a happy, fulfilling life.

There are also women who desire the perfect job, status, power and a man who will let them be who they want to be. Not always easy to find. Granted, some women want much more than others, but if men exchange their power tools for kitchen appliances, are what men and women want so different?

Please note, nowhere in the previous paragraph did I mention the words "Thai or American."

If the stereotypical impression of Thai women is that of petite, demure sex kittens; American women are loud, opinionated, and self-entitled. The truth is, there are women all over the world who fit all of these descriptions. For those willing to put in the time, there are American women every bit as sweet and lovely as Thai women; of course, there are also American women who are bossy feminists, those who are member's of the she-woman man hater's club. Fortunately, Thai feminists are in short supply.

For every Thai woman proclaiming "Thai man no good," there is a Thai boyfriend or husband in an intimate, monogamous and happy relationship. So when a woman says Thai men are no good, don't buy into the bullshit.

The opposite sex has always been a jigsaw puzzle with missing pieces, an area of life I have never quite fully understood, but how many men truly understand the inner workings of women? Do you really want to know everything a woman is thinking and what goes on in a woman's head? Dealing with my own thoughts is difficult enough without worrying about some hormone-fueled nut job who believes all men in her society are bad. I certainly do not want my woman to know everything I think about, do we have to understand everything about everything?

When I was growing up, men were the breadwinners

and women were housewives. The least appealing woman was the stereotypical housewife who loved sitting on the sofa eating chocolate Bon-Bons instead of cooking and cleaning. When the man of the house arrived home, dinner was to be ready and the house spic-and-span.

Even as a young man I knew, if a chick was constantly stuffing her face with Bon-Bons, this was a bad sign of things to come. Millions of western women follow the same path; get married, pop out a couple of rug rats, put on 30-40 pounds, leaving the man to wonder what happened to that phenomenal piece of ass he fell in love with and married.

These days, fat men and women are the norm; men aren't allowed to call their girlfriends or wives fat, for most females consider this cruel and may be grounds for a break-up or divorce, or at least a serious pouting session. Of course, American women call men fat anytime they want and get away with it. TV sitcoms regularly portray men as stupid, fat slobs, who capitulate to their women and rarely say more than "Yes, dear. Whatever you say, dear."

Are Thai woman any different?

The World Health Organization recently reported Thai people are the second fattest in Asia behind Malaysians. So in this way, Thai women are similar to American women. The stereotypical impression of Thai women as small and petite is eroding as their waistlines and hips expand. Just as women come in all shapes and sizes, Thai and American women have similarities and dissimilarities.

Men around the world believe Thai women to be quiet, submissive, and reticent, always giving in to the wishes of their men. They always have their man's favorite breakfast, lunch, and dinner prepared and are happy to give their man a massage, trim his finger and toe nails; as the man, your wish is her command.

A century ago or so, a Thai woman would welcome her husband home from a hard day's work with a cycle of love. Dinner would be waiting, and once they had finished eating, she would run his bath, scrub his back and help him clean those hard to reach places. Then she would give him a traditional Thai massage, knead his tired muscles, and if he so desired, take care of his sexual needs. When the evening was complete and they were ready to sleep, she would kneel at the end of the bed and *wai* her man.

"Thank you, my husband."

Why is a Thai woman so honored to take care of her man? Because she worships the ground he walks on, why else?

The truth is, Thai women may have a greater sense of female responsibility regarding her husband, however, with more females in the Thai workforce, this ritual has become virtually extinct. Not all change is good.

Whether Thai or American, there are women who make great wives and women who make lousy wives. This is common sense, just like there is good and evil in the world. If you marry a prostitute, she might be exactly what you want her to be, as long as you keep up the payments and she doesn't find a bigger, better deal. Hook up with an educated, hard-working woman, and chances are she'll be busy most of the time, and instead of waiting on you hand and foot, she will tell you to go to a salon to get your hair cut, nails clipped, ears cleaned and nose hairs trimmed. When the dinner bell rings, she will complain about how tired she is and instead of a home cooked meal, she will ask you go buy dinner for the both of you.

Thai women have no problem calling people fat, ugly, or whatever else they can think of at the moment, smiling as they insult you. In their opinion, they are not being insulting, they are simply being brutally honest. Despite this, they manage to make their insults sound warm and fuzzy, even cute.

If you have a little twinkle in your eyes, you are moderately successful and polite, take a shower more than once a week, and exude a pleasant odor, finding a Thai woman is easy. The trick is to find a Thai woman as good for you as you are for her, a woman worthy of being your partner.

Thai women and American women tend to want the same things, it is how they go about getting what they want that is different. Thai women may have a certain sweetness and femininity difficult to find in American women, but in the end, they are both still women.

Settling Down

"In the end, it's not the years in your life that count. It's the life in your years."
Abraham Lincoln, 16th president of the United States

***

There comes a time in a man's life when for whatever reason, he gets involved in a serious relationship, eventually taking the plunge and getting married. No matter where you live in the world, marriage is always a dicey prospect, but when finding a female to have sex with is as easy as going to the corner market, it can be even more hazardous. Single men arriving in Thailand often find the women so exotic and different from the women in their own country. If you pay some of them a little money, they go away and leave you to your own vices. It should be so easy with all women.

Thai women, so sweet, so polite, so lovable; how could any man resist? Visiting men with half a brain can and should resist loving them, though, at least until they get to know Thai culture, language and the ways of the women. Instead, lust ruins many a man, leaving them thinking with the little head instead of the big.

The Land of Smiles is full of cheery women with toothy grins, but it is still a poor country, thus some women are willing to use whatever means possible to rise to the next socio-economic level. Hell, women do this in wealthy nations, why wouldn't they do it in the poor ones? After all, "Movin' on Up" or "Doing the George Jefferson" is in every human's DNA.

Making a relationship work with any woman is difficult enough, even when sharing the same culture and background. Add in the language barrier, cultural differences, and financial complications into the mix and making a relationship work with a Thai woman is like playing Russian roulette with a loaded gun.

In the beginning of your time as an expat, learn about the country, the people, the language, and the culture. Learning about Thai culture is like eating a Tootsie Pop. No matter how long you lick it, i.e., gain experience, you never quite reach the chewy Tootsie Roll center. The conundrum is that it is doubtful you will ever discover all the ins and outs of Thai culture. This is understandable, but it is advisable to become acquainted with the rules and the playing field before you attempt to play the game. During this intense knowledge-gathering period, you can start to foster new relationships with more mainstream women. In a land where fulfilling a man's need for sex costs the price of a decent button down shirt, there are no excuses for the forlorn and sexless.

Take as much time as necessary to find your perfect woman, for there is no rush. Use the go-go bars, massage parlors, discos and nightclubs to find temporary companionship. However, make certain that you want a serious relationship because Thai women have a habit of being hard to cast aside once their foot is in the door.

If you are positive you are ready for a serious

relationship, proceed with caution. Despite knowing the pitfalls, one man after another who visits Thailand gets seriously involved with women they barely know, diving in headlong. Sink or swim baby.

Whether you are familiar or unfamiliar with Thai women, or any women, taking it slow is probably the best advice anyone can receive. Getting into a relationship means allowing a woman into your life and into your private affairs. While looking for a woman who is relationship worthy, have fun with the women in beer bars, go-go bars, massage parlors and discotheques.

On a positive note, Thai women make it easy for you to take it slow. If your potential love interest hops in the sack on the first date, odds are she is not quite as innocent as you may think. No one ever is. Not that there is anything wrong with this, but do not kid yourself, Thai culture (like numerous other cultures) generally dictates that Thai women make their man wait a reasonable length of time.

Why do you think there are massage parlors?

While the good Thai women are hesitant to give up the booty, men still crave sex. While waiting for their girl to open her legs, Thai men use massage parlors. Moral argument aside, prostitutes do serve a purpose in society.

While courting, at least in the beginning, Thai women may want to bring a girlfriend along on your first few dates. This means spending more money and having another woman filtering your game, which can quickly become tiresome. When I met my wife, at first she was unwilling to go out with me, with or without friends, and she declined my advances several times. Finally, after much cajoling, she accepted, but only if her two girlfriends joined us. Fortunately though, this seems to be changing, and Thai women nowadays are growing less conservative.

From the woman's perspective, having a friend or friends tag along on a first date and perhaps the second date is brilliant. With a friend, there is a level of safety greater than if she is alone with you, plus her friend can get to know you and voice their opinion. If she has any misgivings about your manipulative male ways or she does not trust herself, having a friend with her provides a temporary buffer zone.

If all goes according to plan, the time will come when the two of you will have your alone time. After this, it's all downhill—just kidding. If you are the sort who likes to party all night, every night, in go-go bars and dance clubs, strolling in at 5 AM, you might want to rethink your quest for a relationship. Be careful what you wish for, you might just get what you want.

Growing Old

"Just remember when you're over the hill, you begin to pick up speed."

Charles M. Schultz, American Cartoonist

***

I

Today is a milestone—I am now 50 years of age. Notice, I did not write 50 years old or 50 years young. I am unsure how I feel about reaching this momentous occasion, thus I will remain neutral.

If I die at 55, life is almost over. With only five years left, I am old and at the end of my life. Should the end come at 75, I have a third of my life left to live. If I manage to make it to 100, I still have half my life remaining. If my time to move on comes in another 50 years, does this make me a youngster? Since we are never certain about the exact time of our death, are we always living at the end of our lives?

When I am 100 years of age, will I be capable of living sans diapers and will my man-parts still function? The answers to these questions make me unwilling to commit to living this long.

Age may only be a number, but it would help if my body knew this. Twenty years past my physical prime, beefier around the middle, and with less hair, I can no

113

longer pass for 30. It had to happen. Part of me refuses to believe I will die one day. Another part embraces the aging process and the certainty of eventual death.

Whether you embrace or fight aging makes no difference, you get older by the second. While diet and exercise can delay the aging process, old age is an undefeated champion. It is best to welcome the inevitable with a smile, fooling it into adding a few extra years.

Age is a state of mind.

Seventy-year-old men in Pattaya go arm in arm with women young enough to be their granddaughters. This facilitates a paradigm shift and makes them feel young again. This may also be why Hugh Hefner is still going strong at eighty-nine.

My ears and nose now need weekly trimming. Miss trimming them and ugly black hairs protrude from my nostrils. Tufts of blonde hair sprout from my ears. Of course, this prompts my always-thoughtful wife to yank them out. When she shaves my head, she also feels the need to shave off any back hair.

"If I don't shave your back, you look like a little gorilla."

There are mornings I wake up ready to run a marathon. I can do anything. Other mornings, I feel like I drank too much Tequila and five angry football players kicked the crap out of me. It is mornings like this when it takes every ounce of my inner strength to lift myself from the bed.

Get up Rocky! You can do it! Drag your lazy, saggy ass out of bed. You are a champion, remember?

I always rise but with each passing year, it takes a little

longer and a little more effort.

II

When I turned 50, I used the phrase 50 years of age. Today, I turned 51 and I will go ahead and say it, I am 51 years old. In the year that has passed, I realized I am no longer getting old—I am old.

My memory is poor and I am forgetful.

I once forgot 5000 baht of just-purchased groceries in the trunk of a taxi. I was almost home when I saw my wife walking on the side of the road with a pair of new shoes and a laptop case. I told the driver to stop, got out, and we walked home together.

As soon as I walked in, my son Nicholas, a connoisseur of everything chocolate, ran up to me.

"Did you remember to get my chocolate milk, Daddy? Where is it, I'm thirsty?"

"Don't worry, I remembered."

I remembered to buy his chocolate milk, I just forgot to bring it in with the groceries.

"Oh shit," I blurted out.

I sprinted out the front door into oncoming traffic. Two blocks away, my groceries were making a U-turn. Our house is on a long, dead-end street and there is only one way out. Disaster averted, but once again, my brain seemed to be firing on less than all cylinders. Maybe this is another sign of aging.

III

On one of my many trips to Cambodia, I awoke at 5AM. I am awake by this time most mornings, but it takes me 2-3 hours to get to the point where I can face the world and start my day. This particular day, I wanted to photograph the sunrise over the Tonle Sap River. I put on a t-shirt and a pair of shorts, grabbed my camera, ran down four flights of stairs, and walked to the river. Two hours later, I had the necessary photos.

I walked over to the Riverside Bistro for an omelet, coffee and toast. My flight to Bangkok left at noon. There was just enough time to eat breakfast, walk back to my room, pack my bags and look over my photographs. A taxi to the airport would take no more than thirty minutes so there was plenty of time.

I walked up the stairs, turned left towards my room, and found the door wide open.

"The maid must be cleaning the room," I thought.

The bed and the room were spotless but the maid was absent.

Why is the door open though, and where are my bags?

I walked back downstairs to the front desk.

"I just went up to my room and my bags are missing. Did you move them?"

"No sir, we do not take our guests bags without permission," she said, emphatically.

"Then where are they?" This was the same receptionist who was ready to cast me out on the street when I arrived. She told me there were no rooms and the system did not reflect my having room reservation. My blood began to boil.

"One moment, sir."

She picked up the telephone, punched in several numbers and waited.

"The foreigner says his bags are missing. I don't know!"

Her voice rose several octaves as she grew more excited.

"Thank you, yes, please! Okay, thank you."

She let out a sigh, put the phone back in its place, turned to me and smiled.

"One moment, sir," she said.

"I didn't tell anyone I was checking out. Where are my bags?"

My frustration grew with each passing second. Then, out of the corner of my eye, I noticed a woman in a uniform walking towards me.

"Sir, please follow her," said the receptionist.

We walked up several flights of stairs before reaching the room. The maid reached into her pocket, pulled out a key and opened the door. As if by magic, my bags and my room reappeared.

"Your room number 403, no 304," she said.

I pulled out my key from my pocket. 4-0-3.

The fourth floor, not third.

"I'm sorry," I said, shaking my head in disbelief.

She forced a smile, closed the door and left me to my thoughts. Stunned, I lay down on my bed. Moments later, there was a knock at my door.

It was the maid—again.

Now what?

I opened the door.

"Sir, you forget," she said, holding up my video camera and tripod.

In my haste to find my bags, I forgot my video camera and tripod in the reception area. She backed away from the door, again forcing a smile. The maid was smiling but I felt like a complete idiot.

IV

The soles of my feet need constant pampering to prevent them from taking on the texture of sandpaper. Every month, without fail, I take a taxi to The Beauty Center off Khao San Road to have the soles of my feet exfoliated. The ritual also prevents the wife from complaining how they look and feel horrible. She complains enough without having to hear her bitch and moan about my feet. The time spent at Khao San Road provides a much needed, albeit brief respite from the monotony of daily life. One visit was different though.

I had a taxi drop me off at the end of Khao San Road, as usual, a ten minute walk from the salon. Khao San Road is a tourist trap, one of many in Bangkok, a short street crammed full of food stalls, bars, coffee shops, tailor shops and vendors selling the usual overpriced crap sold to tourists. A row of parked taxis dot the road, their drivers talking to one another while pursuing potential passengers.

"Boss, you want lady? Beautiful lady? Pattaya?"

"No, thank you, I can find my own."

Sikh tailors stand the middle of the road and are a happy lot. Beware of these friendly fellows.

"My friend, you are a lucky man! Today is your lucky day!"

"Why am I lucky?"

"Please come inside and I will show you!"

Besides working as tailors, on any given day they are also palm readers, capable of seeing the future. For a price, of course. The Sikhs had been a fixture of Khao San Road for many years. Their shtick must work.

The salon opened at noon and it was only 11:30 so I strolled along, taking in the warmth of the sun before stopping at an ATM to make a withdrawal. I took out 3000 baht, then walked to the salon, said my hellos and laid back in one of the chairs.

Finally, I can relax.

The girl assigned to my feet put them in a bowl of warm water, scrubbing them with a pumice stone before beginning the massage. Slow and deep, sliding up my legs and along the pressure points, then down to the soles of my feet, working my flesh like a baker kneading dough. I was in heaven, if only for five minutes. Something felt odd, out of place.

Where's my wallet?

My pockets were empty. My phone and keys were sitting on a small table to the left. No wallet.

Maybe I was sitting on it.

I raised up. Nothing. I looked on the floor. Only hair and dirt. I walked outside and looked along the path I took to the salon. Again, nothing.

I left my wallet at the ATM with my AMEX card still in the machine.

Shit!

The foot lady sensed something was wrong.

"What's the problem?" she asked.

"I think I lost my wallet."

"Shit, how can I pay the salon?"

I reached inside my pocket and found a measly 300 baht. The foot scrub and pedicure cost 500 baht and I always gave a 150-baht tip. Plus, I still needed to get home.

"I don't have enough money," I said, with my most sympathetic look. The last thing I wanted to do was call the wife to bring me some cash. She was working and my forgetfulness would take at least three hours out of her day. Of course, I would never hear the end of it.

They knew they were getting their money one way or another.

"I'm going to see if I can find my wallet, okay?"

"No problem," she said.

It was a problem for me though. I was positive I made the withdrawal on Khao San Road. As hard as I tried though, I was unable to remember the location of the ATM where I made the withdrawal. Panic set in. I walked along the main road, into the alleyways, and even checked with the police station set up to help hapless foreigners like myself. Still, nothing.

Why was I so forgetful? Was something wrong with me? Are the wires fried in my brain or am I losing my mind?

My AMEX card, two ATM cards connected to my US bank accounts, all my Thai ATM cards and three thousand baht—gone. I called American Express, and two hours later, a courier arrived with a replacement card. I walked across the street from the salon to the nearest ATM, careful to remember to retrieve my new card, withdrew another three thousand baht, and paid the salon. To this day, I have been unable to remember where I withdrew the money.

V

A month after losing my wallet at Khao San Road, I left my wallet in a taxi.

Three days after shelling out 5900 baht to have my iPhone replaced, I left it in the back seat of a taxi. I loved that phone. Now someone else loves it.

When I go to the mall, I sometimes find myself standing inside the entrance wondering why I was there. Where I was going? What was the reason for my being there? Did I need to pay a bill or buy something? Was it important? Which way should I go? Whenever this happens, I will take fifteen minutes and have an espresso. Usually this is long enough to jog my memory.

Perhaps it is information overload. Maybe I smoked too much marijuana when I was younger. Maybe I have too much on my mind. For twenty years I took punches and kicks to the head. This coupled with twice falling on my head seems to have taken a toll. One of my doctors informed me Alzheimer's disease might be in my future.

There are days I sit at my computer, attempting to write. Nothing comes out, my thoughts jumbled and slow. I do not have writer's block, but I am unable to arrange my thoughts. Whatever the reason, absentmindedness, forgetfulness and confusion tax my existence.

Ernest Hemingway used to stand when he wrote. I believe I now understand why. If you sit down, it takes energy to get up. I am only 53 but rising after a long sit can be a slow, painful process. Nobody tells you this will happen when you are young.

The other day at Starbucks, I met a well-spoken, older Thai man. He once worked as an engineer in Huntington Beach, California, where I lived for several years. We talked for 30 minutes or so and in the course of our conversation, he informed me he was 70 years old and retired. He had no problem using the word old and had come to terms with being on the downside of the mountain.

Then, he took a long, deep breath, let out a long sigh, and drifted off for a few moments, lost in thought.

"You okay?" I asked.

"Yes," he said.

He turned and looked at me.

"I hope my wife gets here soon. I am tired," he said.

"Maybe you should have another coffee," I told him.

"No, no," he said. "I am tired because I am old."

"Here I am a young man," he said, pointing to his heart. "But I am an old man."

My father once told me he started feeling his age at forty. He is now 73 and well-preserved. Although twenty years younger than my father, I have accumulated far more injuries. I can only imagine how I will feel when I hit 70. Maybe like the man I met at Starbucks. Young heart, old body, and far more tired than I feel at 53.

Observations On Aging

"How old would you be if you didn't know how old you was?"

Satchel Paige, Baseball Player

***

Compare the words aging or elderly with youth and vibrancy. Which do you prefer?

When I was in my teens, I had the attitude that I was different from everyone else. Old people were old because they were weak mentally. Aging got the better of them because they allowed it to get the better of them. I decided I'd be an anomaly and stay alive for as long as I damn well pleased.

Without any formal training, I ran a 4:30 mile simply by sprinting from start to finish. When I started getting serious about boxing and martial arts, only then did I start running regularly. Before training started, I would run three or four miles and jump rope for 30 minutes straight. In addition, once a week I ran a 6.6-mile course, up and down hills in the blistering California desert heat. My personal best was forty-one minutes.

Injuries were rare when I was young. Dying never occurred to me. In my mind, I was invincible, a real-life Superman. Nothing could stop me. In my younger days, I could drink all night, take a cold shower and go to work without a hangover. Now, I prefer sleeping to partying and rarely drink. Just the thought of a hangover is enough to limit my intake.

When I was in my teens and early twenties, I went to the mall with my friends, always on the lookout for women willing to give up their phone numbers. Now when I go to the mall, I put my headphones on, ignore everyone, get what I need, and come home.

I used to look at myself in the mirror and think, "Damn, I look good!" Now I look in the mirror and spend the next ten minutes trying to convince myself I still look good for my age. Wrinkles add character. Baldness is a sign of strength and manliness. If this is true, why do I wish I had more hair and fewer wrinkles?

I bought bottles of Pepe Lopez or Jose Cuervo Tequila, downed the entire bottle with friends before going out on the town, and then drank more in the bar. Now if I buy a bottle of Tequila, it lasts for a year, or longer.

As a bachelor, I lived in a studio apartment because it was cheap, easy to clean and I was rarely home. On the rare occasion I was home, the bed was the focal point of the room. If I had a female visitor, there was an excellent chance we would end up in bed. A studio apartment made getting laid easy. Now I need a bigger place to live because I spend the majority of my time at home. My wife and I need space to breathe. We have a large bed and can stretch out without falling off the bed or having to lay on top of one another. If we lived in a studio apartment now, we would drive each other crazy.

One forgettable day, I woke up with a few niggling aches and pains. A week later, they were still there. When my hair started receding, I thought it was because I wore a motorcycle helmet every day. Wrong. Then I noticed that I was tiring faster and the injuries from my twenties were piling up. The injuries following me into my thirties and forties reminded me of the old days. Finally, I accepted that what I was feeling were the first signs of aging.

Growing old is a journey of self-discovery. It has taken me 50 years to realize that when I was young, I knew less than I thought. Now that I am older, I think before I speak and I take my time making decisions. I know more, but I am smart enough to know there is a lot I do not know. The elderly have more life experience and know there is always much to learn. By the time a person figures this out, life is almost over.

For 500 years, people have been searching for the *Fountain of Youth*. Do people search for the *Fountain of Elderly*? If getting old is so great, why does Hugh Hefner have young girlfriends and not old? Is his main squeeze an 85-year-old he keeps tucked away from inquiring minds?

When a forty-year-old cashier at the grocery store calls you sir, you know you are old. You know you're old when a big night out on the town means going to a coffee shop for a muffin and espresso.

I am now living in Thailand on a retirement visa. According to the Thai government, enough of my life is over to warrant a retirement visa. Maybe I'm I closer to the grave than I think.

Gravity is an enemy who cares not who you are but whether you exercise enough to give it a good fight. Once I hit 50, gravity started winning the battle.

According to Pfizer and Lilly, the manufacturers of Viagra and Cialis, the average age of the men purchasing their products is in the mid-fifties. Their commercials will be targeting me in a few short years.

In my 60's and 70's, Depends adult diapers will set their sights on me. Could this be the genesis of the phrase, The Golden Years?

I used to look forward to the major events to come. Now the little things in life are more important. A morning cup of coffee, an afternoon cup of tea, and a good meal with friends are some of the little things that make life worth living. I forget what this has to do with the aging process, though.

Children force you to grow up and change your life. Those without children may think they understand life and all it encompasses, but the truth is that having children teaches a person more than they learn on their own.

My sons never let me forget that in their eyes I am old.

When I tell them, "My back hurts," they ask, "Is it because you're old?"

"How old are you Daddy?"

"Fifty," I say.

"Wow, you are old."

A Thai friend once told me his mother was an old woman.

"How old is she?" I asked.

"She is very old. Fifty-two."

Perhaps he was trying to tell me something.

My wife recently asked if I think we will still be having sex when I am 70.

"Why not?" I asked.

"Ewwww... really?"

This is exactly what I needed to hear.

Growing old means exercising care when passing gas. Need I say more?

How much longer until I have that old person smell? Or do I already smell old?

The older I get, the less I care what people think of me. People have the right to like or dislike me and vice versa. If they don't like me, fuck 'em. After all, what is not to like?

We can choose how and where we live and what we do with our lives. We can choose to face impending death with a smile or go kicking and screaming. I choose to smile while giving death the middle finger and calling it a motherfucker.

Scott Mallon

Paradise

"Paradise was always over there, a day's sail away. But it's a funny thing, escapism. You can go far and wide and you can keep moving on and on through places and years, but you never escape your own life. I, finally, knew where my life belonged. Home."

J. Maarten Troost, Author

***

When I made the move to Thailand, I was 33 years-old and ready for an adventure. After several trips to the country, I was certain I had found paradise. One day I woke up and something clicked. I wanted more out of my life. I wanted to see the world, to start anew, and I wanted to do it my way. Thailand was like no other place I had seen and seemed like the ideal place to do so.

My initial plan was to stay for one year and get to know myself again, sans stress. This was twenty years ago, when smartphones and internet technology were in their infancy and had yet to make the world smaller. Time provides insight and change, and I am much different from the person I was when I arrived in Thailand.

Although I am happy with my decision to move abroad, I would be hesitant to make the same move at my current age and in my current situation.

When I made the move, the time was right. I was still a young man and had little to lose. If I failed, there was plenty of time to get back on track. The people in Thailand were charming, friendly, and open to foreigners and the country had yet to become the cliché backpacker's destination. Bars were open all night, go-go dancers pranced around naked, and tourists willing to give anything for a beautiful piece of ass had yet to corrupt the working girls.

Still, Thailand was and is no paradise. Once you have lived here and the magic of the relationship has calmed like the morning after a fierce night of drinking, you realize like any other place, the country has its share of flaws.

Every so often, fate grants temporary access to paradise. The allure of paradise, even the idea of it, is strong and irresistible, like heroin minus the devastating side effects. Once experienced, the chase is on. Some remain stuck in a routine, never getting the slightest glimpse of the alternative to their mundane existence. The thought that life could be worse acts as a pacifier for others.

Now older and slightly wiser, I have concluded lasting paradise is void of reality, a figment of our imaginations. Paradise is fleeting. The concept of paradise runs deep in all of us though, in some peaceful, faraway land surrounded by all that is beautiful and full of joy and laughter.

When paradise and reality collide, reality always triumphs. Reality is daily chores, traffic jams, screaming children, alimony, child support, boredom, drugs, alcohol, smiling at people you dislike, talking to people you do not want to talk to, agreeing when you would rather disagree and working for a living. Reality is truth. The cruel realization is that there is no paradise, at least not in the purest definition.

Once entrenched in a foreign country, an exotic destination morphs into a place called home. Normalcy and the mundane replace the euphoria of the vacation, of the temporary. When on holiday, one must never lose sight of the fact that living in a country foreign to your own is different from vacationing in one.

Many years ago, I spent three weeks in Cannes, France. Oh, how I loved Cannes. The French were not rude. This was a myth!

The Cannes lifestyle was right up my alley. Every morning, I threw on a sports jacket, took a leisurely stroll to one of the many cafés in the city center, ate a buttery croissant, and sipped espresso. At lunch, my friends and I patronized the coolest place we could find, devouring French food and laughing at all the miserable schmucks stuck in the daily grind. Occasionally, in an attempt to look more important than we were, we went to the luxurious Carlton Hotel — where anyone who is anyone hangs out — all for the privilege of paying $20 for a cappuccino. At night, we dined in fine restaurants and partied until the wee hours of the night. Twice we lucked our way on to yachts owned by someone whose name we did not know.

For a brief period, the south of France was one of the most magnificent places on earth. Before long I thought, "I want to live here!".

I had to find a way to make it my home. I was in a beautiful place surrounded by beautiful people and I was sure this was the life for me. What a life! *C'est magnifique!*

Alas, paradise was temporary, even in Cannes.

They Call Me Farang

A week into the trip I rented a cellular phone. Not the brightest move on my part, but I was walking the red carpet and wanted to call my friends to gloat a little. I found a little shop near where I was staying and within 30 minutes, I had a phone.

The luxury of having the phone was costly. The deposit was $400 and after adding phone time, and sales tax, the bill came to just over $500. This was fine, I had $1200 in my checking account and as long as I did not lose the phone, I would get my deposit back. At most, I would spend $100-$200 more for phone calls. Later that day, after realizing I was low on cash, I walked to the local ATM. I punched in my password, requested the equivalent of $500, and hit withdrawal.

Denied! Denied! Denied! You have insufficient funds to complete this transaction.

What? *Pardonne-moi?* There must be some mistake. Or a computer glitch. What is wrong with this machine? I just checked my account balance! I slammed my fingers on the machine's buttons and out popped a grimy slip of paper.

Your balance is $200. You are a loser. Go home foreigner, you are poor; Cannes is only for the wealthy.

Lucky for me I had my overpriced phone. I called customer service at my bank, who moments later informed me that the friendly little Frenchman at the mobile phone shop had double charged me. Accidentally, of course.

This was not good, for time in paradise requires cash.

I walked back to the store and explained the situation.

Now, in paradise, the smiling Frenchman would say, "Hello my friend, *Oui, Oui,* so sorry, let me get your refund *tout de suite.*"

But this was reality.

"No! I no double charge you, sir!"

"But my bank… it said you… maybe there was a mistake?"

"No!

"Are you sure?" I asked.

"NO MISTAKE!" he said, slamming his fist on the counter.

I gave up, walked outside, called my bank again, and informed them paradise had betrayed me. Dejected, I walked back to the house I was renting. I went online and filled out my bank's dispute form. My bank was in the good ole U.S.A. and while the country might not be paradise, at least my bank had my back. In seconds, they credited my account with the disputed funds.

The Frenchman would not defeat me.

My holiday ended, as holidays always do, and I flew back home to Thailand.

Paradise still fresh in my mind, I dreamed of my new life in France.

When I first thought of moving to Cannes, I knew the cost of living would be prohibitive. Still, I sat down and crunched the numbers. Had I been single, I could have found a hostel or some other cheap accommodation. Living out of a backpack was not my idea of fun though and with a wife and two kids in tow, we would need a higher standard of living.

Looking back, the thought of living in Cannes seems silly. Would moving to France after a three-week vacation be worth the risk to my family? Perhaps if I were sitting on a fat bank account, where money was not an issue, but my account balance was pitiful.

Do three weeks in France necessitate picking up everything and moving there? No more than a night in the sack with a sexy Thai stripper obliges a man to marry her.

Cannes is a fantastic place to visit but far from paradise. Living there would be much more difficult than I first thought, logistically and financially. If I found a more appealing destination, would I then ask my family to pick up and move again?

What makes Thailand so enticing? Much like Tahiti, Bora Bora, or any other dream destination, it is the illusion of paradise that makes a destination beguiling. Paradise on earth exists for those willing to ignore the failings and imperfections of a particular destination.

Crystal-clear beaches, smiling, happy people, sunny days and balmy nights can quickly turn into polluted, overpriced tourist traps. One day you notice the sun is no longer shining, it rains more than you like, the beach is less than pristine, and xenophobic attitudes surround you. Then it hits you; paradise has blemishes, imperfect like a fine broad with a big honkin' zit on her ass. You take it anyway, zit, shit, and all.

Paradise is where and what you want it to be, and most of the time, it lies between the ears. If you find it, let me know, I want in.

Scott Mallon
Shades of Green

"Diligence is the mother of good luck"

Benjamin Franklin,
Founding Father of the United States of America

***

I wake up without an alarm clock. I do not own one. I have nowhere in particular to go, no job to rush off to, and yet, I am awake by 4:30 AM every day of my life. Time is money, but time is also a limited resource and our most precious commodity. I need only charge my batteries so I may function; I can sleep when I die. I go to sleep when I am tired, taking catnaps in the middle of the day and, when necessary, I knock out early in the evening. Then I wake at midnight, only to repeat the process a few hours later. I do not punch a clock, however, my time clock is much less forgiving.

There are people who tell me I am living the life, or they wish they were in my position. "Thailand! Wow!"

Perhaps this is one reason viewers like my YouTube videos; they have the opportunity to live vicariously through me. When I talk about Thailand, they are there. I give the good, the bad, and the ugly, and this makes it *real*. Those who have visited the country can relate.

My wife knows better. She knows I always want more, I always want something different. Rarely am I satisfied and I am always pursuing something. No matter my location, I am restless and ready to go somewhere. Traveling, seeing and photographing the world, and my family, are what makes me happy. In my mind, I am always in transition. I am still trying to figure out exactly what it is I am after. Perhaps Ayahuasca would help — experiencing the effects of it is at the top of my bucket list.

I set aside time to write — yet most of what I write remains unseen and often ends up in the trash. I set aside time to take photos. Like writing, this is an artistic outlet and one that keeps me somewhat sane. Note the word "somewhat". We are all crazy in our own way.

I finally got around to counting my photos. There are several hundred thousand. I rarely make time to upload them to my website nor do I display the vast majority of them.

People often tell me, "You're a good photographer. Why don't you try selling your photos?"

I do sell some of them. The truth is I have come to realize I take photos for myself, not for anyone else. Sure, it is nice to have people enjoy what you do and to pay you for our efforts but I care more about what *I* want. Call me selfish.

Some say I am lucky; I am living the dream. I think otherwise. Luck happens when preparation and opportunity meet. I found my way, with a little help from my friends, and I knew where I was and where I wanted to go. Luck had little to do with this. Luck is winning the lottery. Luck comes into play when one takes great risk, prepares to the best of their ability, wins the lottery, or lightning strikes them instead of the person next to them (bad luck).

The older I get, the more I learn about the many flaws of human beings. In my 52 years of life, I have concluded that the only thing important and altruistic is caring for others. Preparing our children to live without us and to interact and live in harmony with others is my way.

Eleanor Roosevelt once said, "With freedom comes responsibility."

I am still attempting to figure out my responsibilities other than making certain my family is happy, healthy, and well fed.

If others deem our achievements important, we may remember them for a few decades. How many kids nowadays know of Albert Einstein or the Wright brothers? Do teenagers know Guglielmo Marconi or Alexander Graham Bell? Perhaps if they pulled their noses from their smart phones they might know, but the truth is, the *person* is unimportant. It is the achievement that we tend to remember.

Nowadays people go out to dinner and refrain from engaging in conversation. Too busy texting on their cell phones or playing Angry Birds; they are on autopilot. Shoppers walk through malls like zombies, heads down, eyes glued to their phones. Society and social media serve a purpose, yet when abused, they shackle human beings until they no longer know who they are or what is important.

When confronted by one of these cell phone zombies, I stick out my elbow, accidentally, of course, in an effort to knock some sense into them and force them to revert to the manual mode. My wife once sold her iPhone to me because she thought it too complicated for a phone. She now uses it to do business, so much so I implemented a rule banning phones during family time. It is difficult for her to adhere to this rule. Without her phone, she is walking naked in public.

We often take people for granted, even those who are historic figures. This makes them no less important to people, though. The day will come when consumers will forget Bill Gates, Steve Jobs, and Richard Branson. Think about it. Steve Wozniak... who's he? Humans have limited memories and tend to remember only what is important and pressing. The previously stated entrepreneurs are unimportant. What they accomplished is what is important.

Society may remember those involved in something truly momentous or historic for several hundred centuries: George Washington, Attila the Hun, Genghis Khan, Marco Polo, Christopher Columbus. Perhaps we will remember Bill Gates, however, when people sit down at their personal computer, are they thinking of Bill Gates?

Often, I sit and think. This is more than can be said for some people who simply live their lives in a perpetual state of unconsciousness. My brain resides firmly between my ears and I intend to continue using it as long as I can. I keep hoping something exceptional, something monumental, will spring forth. So far, the best I have been able to come up with is cool, unique, and different. Nothing exceptional, though.

Notice there is nothing in the above text containing the word Thailand. This is intentional.

Why, might you ask? After all, Thailand is a fantastic place. Correct?

Most of the time.

Thailand is simply a huge piece of land inhabited at this time by a decent group of people. I have traveled to numerous, similar plots of land in my life, and although I like Thailand, I am, and always will be, nomadic by nature and faithful to my plot of land. There are positives and negatives no matter where you live and Thailand is no different.

The grass is supposedly always greener on the other side. The trick is to get to the other side and leave before the greener grass begins fading. You move on to greener pastures and continue the process. After 20 years in the green grass, though, almost everything fades a little. Even in Thailand.

Life could be much worse, though. No matter how disgruntled, irritated, befuddled, or discombobulated I become, I always keep this in mind.

"It could be much worse."

I could be living in a slum or war zone. I could be starving. Instead of writing inside the serenity of my home, at my local Starbucks, or traveling to another special piece of land, I could be fighting for my life, vying to escape beheading at the hands of medieval animals hell-bent on cramming their idiotic ideology down my throat.

Luck is being born on the plot of land known as the United States, to loving parents. The rest, I did on my own.

Looking Ahead

"Things do not change; we change."
Henry David Thoreau, American essayist, poet and philosopher

***

Curiosity occasionally prompts me to ask myself '*What if?*'

What if I had turned left instead of right? What if I stayed put instead of going forward? What if I had continued living in the United States, working as a printing broker, met an American woman and lived out my remaining years there? What if I had decided to move to Japan or Mexico or the Netherlands instead of Thailand? What if I just took an extended vacation? How would my life be different?

I will never know. Although we can never go back in time, we all do have crystal balls that provide a glimpse into the future. If we murder another human being or rob a bank, we know there is a good chance we will end up in prison. If we down a bottle of Tequila in ten minutes, we get stinking drunk. We can figure out the solution: if I do A, B happens.

Life will always be full of unanswered questions, unsolved riddles, and *what ifs*. The past is the past and preparing for the future is all we can do. Then fate takes over.

Scott Mallon

It's been nearly 20 years since I moved to Thailand and I still enjoy living here. Life has been good. Over the years, numerous people have asked if I think I will live in Thailand *forever*. When I first moved here, I was positive I would never again live in America. Thailand was heaven on earth and the very thought of moving back to the United States brought on cold sweats. It takes a good year in a country before one can see past the smiles and polite behavior though, and eventually, I learned perceptions are in a perpetual state of flux.

One of the most common statements I hear from foreigners, almost always coming from someone with limited knowledge of the country, is that Thailand is paradise. The truth is, Thailand is like anywhere else; there are positives and negatives. Fortunately, there are still more positives than negatives.

There are beautiful beaches.

They are beautiful, but most are overdeveloped. Some are indeed beautiful, others are polluted.

The people are wonderful.

Yes, on the whole they are polite and friendly. Just like anywhere though, there are good and bad people, and people somewhere in between. The majority of Thais are decent and gracious hosts but some haven't got a clue of what racism is nor do they care what anyone thinks. That is, unless it affects their tourism.

You live here 20 years? Now you are Thai people.

No, I'm not, and I never will be. I will always be an American in Bangkok; a foreigner, an immigrant, an expat. I will never be Thai.

I would love to work in Thailand.

The job market is extremely competitive and people from all around the world want to live in Thailand. You need to be a hustler or someone with unusual skills for jobs are scarce — unless you want to work as an English teacher.

Thailand is an awesome place to live.

Thailand is a great place to visit, a short-term paradise. Living in Thailand is different from visiting though, but if you stay based in reality, keep your expectations in check and understand the culture is different from your own, it can be an excellent place to hang your hat. Then again, there are many fantastic places in the world to live. Think about it. There is no single perfect place, no country that is the magical cure-all for one's woes. Living in Thailand is like having a mischievous dog; he may dig holes in your backyard or chew on your shoes but you still love him.

What advice would I give someone looking to move to Thailand or elsewhere?

Figure out if moving to Thailand is what you truly want to do. Dedicate a full year to getting to know your possible future home. You will be away from your family and friends, your home, your culture, and all that is familiar and you will be always be *the foreigner.*

Moving to Thailand is simple. Make the decision to give it a try, save as much money as possible, and get on a plane. Staying in Thailand is slightly more difficult. You'll need to wade through the language and cultural barriers, visa requirements, and unless you are independently wealthy or retired, earn an income. There may be times when you question the move; remain resilient and committed but draw a line and know when to say enough is enough. We have become spoiled and soft and expect too much to come with little effort. When the slightest problem arises, there is a tendency to panic.

After two years in Thailand, I ran out of money and began teaching English. I hated it but earned enough to pay my rent and utilities and to feed myself. I tried everything I knew at the time to earn more money but could not crack the code. Perpetually broke and growing more miserable with each passing day, I decided enough was enough and made arrangements to fly back to the US. I chose to give Seattle a try. In less than a week, found a month-long temp job as a paper cutter. The company gave me two options; relocate to the Oregon plant or find another job. I found work on a fishing boat in Alaska. After three months on the Bering Sea, I saved $10,000. I flew back to Thailand. It became apparent the money would not last. With no way to earn a living in Thailand, I decided to go back to Alaska. I hated the work but I saved more money and by the time I flew back to Thailand, I figured out that the internet was the answer to my dilemma. Countless explorers found their destinations, then built a life for themselves in a foreign land with far less than we have at our disposal in this era. With the internet, we can teach ourselves to speak languages, chart a path across the equator, learn how to fix cars and motorcycles and even figure out what to do in case of an illness. Along the way, life will knock you backwards or stop you dead in your tracks; nevertheless, the trick is to keep trying. No matter what, keep thinking about a solution and try anything with a remote chance of success.

With age comes wisdom and if I had it to do all over again, the one thing I would have done more religiously is save money. Save your money. Sacrifice a little now for security in a future.

Success or failure is all up to you.

Am I an expatriate or an immigrant?

Both. I can deal with most of Thailand's negatives but there is one negative that constantly has me considering life back in the United States — if you are a foreigner living in Thailand, *you will never be Thai*. Although this is one of the reasons I moved to the country, I failed to understand the significance of these five words. I am no different from Mexican, Cuban, Thai, Chinese, or other immigrant in the United States; as an American in Thailand, I have always been aware of this but it took time to understand that no matter how long I have lived here, they will always call me *farang*.

If I knew then what I know now, would I do it all over again?

Hell yeah! I would do it for the adventure, the rollercoaster ride into the unknown, for the thrill of experiencing life in a country so foreign to my own.

Do I think I'll live in Thailand for the rest of my life?

Looking ahead, it now seems unlikely. I will probably always spend a few months out of the year here though, for as I previously stated, I still enjoy my life in Thailand. Being married to a Thai woman and having two children though, we have accumulated a container of household goods. Moving back to the United States would be costly and a massive undertaking and our children are still in school. We are planning for the future and at some point, maybe five years, maybe ten, once our sons have finished high school, we will probably begin living in the U.S, at least part-time.

I love Thailand but love America more. I am and always will be, an American. There are those who leave America because they are sick of politics and the direction they see their country headed. Others leave because they get more value for the dollar in Thailand or they feel the American dream died decades ago. It sounds cliché, but I am proud to be an American. I left because I wanted an adventure. There's been wine, women, song, sex, travel, language, culture, and I have seen a fair amount of the world. And I'm still traveling.

I got action and I got adventure. In some instances, I got more than I bargained for. Along the way, there were interactions with a host of crazy characters I might not have met back home. It's been a wild ride so far, who knows; maybe I'll be here another 20 years. I am an American and I will die as one. As unimportant as this may seem, I want America to be my final resting place. End of story. Thank you and good night.

Ten Things Learned from Living in Thailand

"Come with more money than you think you need and spend less than you think you should."

Scott Mallon

***

One reason why I have always loved traveling and seeing the world is because doing so provides you with the opportunity to learn about the world firsthand. Stay curious and continue learning and no matter how old you are, you retain the will to live. Once the desire to learn stops, the mind dies. Then the spirit dies and finally, the body gives out and dies.

Below are ten of the many things I have learned so far from living in Thailand. This list is far from comprehensive nor is it exclusive to Thailand.

1. Count on yourself - good parents strive to make their children self-reliant. Seeing Thais struggle in daily life opened my eyes and showed me just how hard it is for some to provide food, clothing and shelter. Life is a constant battle, and while asking for help or guidance is okay in some circumstances, self-reliance remains foremost. I prefer to stay in a hotel than couch surf. I prefer to buy and use my own products as opposed to borrowing. When I am financially sound enough, one of my goals is to live off the grid, at least partially. This means using solar for power, rain catchers for water, and gas or wood for heat and fire. While I am fortunate and have others I can count on in a pinch, I prefer to rely on myself. If something goes wrong, I only have myself to blame.

2. Saying nothing speaks volumes - silence is golden. When I was young, I felt the need to respond verbally or physically if wronged. Doing nothing is an action and sometimes, doing or saying absolutely nothing, smiling, or completely ignoring a situation, speaks volumes. Respond or take action only when necessary and useful.

I have a tendency to put my foot in my mouth and get in trouble when I speak out of emotion. There is a time and place to speak your mind and times to keep your mouth shut. The experienced adult knows when to speak and when to bite their tongue.

3. Mai Pen Rai - this Thai phrase encompasses a philosophy of life. It has several meanings when translated; never mind, take it easy, everything is okay; everything will be okay, keep smiling and don't worry. When things are not going the way you want them to or times are tough, *Mai Pen Rai* has taught me that for better or worse, everything will work out. A situation might work out differently than I prefer, but worrying accomplishes very little and is a waste of energy.

Now if I have a problem, instead of obsessing, I allot a set period of time, perhaps 10-15 minutes, to contemplate the severity of the problem and to think of the solutions. Once this time is up, I mentally put the problem in a box and file it away until I choose to pull it back out.

4. Think long term - When I lived in the US, I thought a week, a month, perhaps a year or two in advance. Now I tend to think five or ten years in advance. Thinking long-term can be beneficial in a variety of ways; today's actions are a crystal ball into the future. When interacting with others, remember that like it or not, those people may still be around in 10 or 20 years. There have been several occasions when I said or did something I should not have, and it later came back to bite me on the behind. Choose your words carefully.

5. Money is important, but it is not everything and can't buy love

Money can rent a body but it cannot buy love. Money provides stability and options, it can make life easier, but there is no guarantee it will buy happiness. Would you rather earn a comfortable living working at a job you enjoy immensely or work at a job you hate bringing in a huge salary? There is always a tradeoff, for money rarely comes easily.

Want a wife? Show women you have a fat bank account and they'll come running out from places you had no idea existed. Choose the woman who will still be around if by chance you lose your fortune and who is willing to work alongside you instead of living off what you earn.

6. Everything is not always as it seems

If saying nothing at all speaks volumes, perhaps it is helpful to remember that while we are looking at the world one way, others might be looking at it in a completely different way.

Have you ever lost your keys, searched everywhere for

them, and were unable to find them?

Later, you find they were in one of your pockets or on a table right in front of you? Think of all the angles, not just your own. Perhaps what you think is black is actually dark blue.

As Bruce Lee said in the movie, *Enter the Dragon*, "Don't concentrate on the finger or you will miss all of the heavenly glory."

7. Family comes first - Family is the bedrock upon which Thai society rests, and while family has always been important to me, moving here taught me that my family needs to be a priority and we could be closer. Thai society teaches children to honor and respect their parents. I have heard children whine and cry, but rarely have I heard one talk back to an adult. Children may live with their parents well past the age of 18, often marrying and then moving the wife in as part of the extended family. Often, several generations of family members live together under one roof, even one room!

When my wife and I explain to our sons that one day they will go out into the world, find a job, live on their own, marry, and have children, their response is always the same, "That's fine, but we like living with you, we don't want to move out."

This may change as we all grow older, but until living in Thailand, I would have never thought my children would voluntarily want to live with us.

8. Respect your elders

The elderly are a valuable resource with a wealth of information to bestow upon the younger generation. Unlike

American culture, Thai culture respects and reveres the elderly, even worships them, and it is rare for a family to put their loved one in a rest home.

As my father used to tell me, "Big fish don't get big by being stupid."

Paralleling this same line of thought, the elderly did not grow old without learning a thing or two. We need to respect our elders, if not for any other reason than they have managed to survive longer than we have and might have something to offer.

9. A smile goes a long way

It sounds so cliché but smiling costs nothing. Smiling also makes you feel better and lightens the mood, opening the door to conversation and friendship. When I first came to Thailand, I was leery of others. I was ready to fight if I thought someone did something inappropriate.

Thailand and working as a photographer has taught me this was my way of overcompensating for my own fears. Smiling goes a long way, often diffusing tension and putting people at ease.

10. We all want the same thing

We all want the same thing; a roof over our head, enough food to eat, a decent education, a loving family, fulfilling relationships, a better life for our children and health and happiness.

While Thais and foreigners generally want the same things, what makes us different is the method we use to get what we are after. As I like to say, the wiring in Thais and Westerners is different. Of course, there are aspects of foreign cultures I dislike or disagree with, but as long as people are not harming others with their actions, how they live their lives is their business.

Cheat Sheet

"Common sense is the most widely shared commodity in the world, for every man is convinced that he is well supplied with it."

René Descartes

***

Common sense is an important attribute to have wherever you are in the world, thus, much of what you need to know and remember while in Thailand is common sense. For some reason though, common sense is one of the first things men forget when they come to Thailand. The words of wisdom in this chapter can be applied just about anywhere in the world and while I am certain those reading this book are endowed with common sense, nevertheless, I suggest you read it anyway. If one of these items jogs your memory at a later date, it might very well save you time, money, and even your life.

If you can't say something nice, don't say anything at all—especially when it comes to the King and Royal Family. Never speak ill of the monarchy, even in jest.

Lèse-majesté is the legal definition of an offense that violates the dignity of a ruler as the representative of a sovereign power. Making disparaging comments about the King of Thailand and the Royal Family, even in jest, is one of the easiest ways of taking up involuntary residence at the Bangkok Hilton. The number of Lèse-majesté cases filed

151

has increased dramatically in recent years, with foreigners representing a handful of those imprisoned. If you value your freedom, keep your mouth shut and your opinions to yourself.

Do not overstay, ever!

There are a myriad of excuses for overstaying, but the bottom line is overstaying is like telling the teacher the dog ate your homework. The only reason for a person to overstay is if they are physically unable to renew or extend their visa. Even this is unpardonable as most hospitals will handle visa matters for their patients. Forgetfulness, laziness, being too busy, and a lack of funds are all unacceptable reasons for overstaying.

The current fine for overstaying is 500 baht per day up to a maximum of 20,000 baht. You know when your visa expires, thus it is your responsibility to make certain you renew your visa or leave the country before overstaying. If you have a problem and are concerned with overstaying, go to your local immigration office. The majority of the time they can and will help.

You will never be Thai.

Once you have lived in Thailand for a few years and you master the basics of the Thai language, someone will inevitably comment on your skill.

"You speak Thai very well! Now you are Thai people."

If you were Thai, the government would charge you the same price to enter a national park. There would be no two-tiered pricing.

You will be welcomed by Thais, you will make friends with Thais, but make no mistake, you will never be Thai.

Respect the Thai national anthem

Any time you hear the national anthem while in Thailand, stand up if you're sitting and stand still if you're moving. The Thai anthem is always played in theaters prior to the start of a movie. Stand up or suffer the consequences.

Learn the rules of the game and how to play it

Look at living in Thailand as a game of chess. You can't play chess or checkers before learning the rules of the game. Learn as many of the rules of the game as you can before visiting or moving to Thailand and once here, make it your business to learn the rest as quickly as possible.

There is a huge difference between visiting and living in Thailand

Before deciding Thailand is the place for you, visit the country for three to six months, preferably a full year. Consider the first year a probationary period. Give yourself enough time to transform from tourist to expat. Once the blinders are off and the initial love affair with the country has mellowed, then finalize your decision.

The 7 Ps

The 7 P's is a military adage that stands for proper planning and preparation prevents piss-poor performance. Shit happens. If you're planning on living in Thailand you need to be prepared. Have a financial back-up plan and an escape plan. The best laid plans often go awry and despite doing your best, there may come a time when the smartest option is to pack up and go home. At the very least, you should have the money to purchase an airline ticket home.

If It Seems Too Good to Be True, It Probably Is

This applies anywhere in the world. In Thailand, there

is a tendency to talk things up.

"It's beautiful!"

"Special price for you!"

"It's not expensive."

"Your family will love this place."

If you're fortunate, everything will be as stated. Do your due diligence beforehand; make certain you receive what is due.

"Wow, only 100 baht for this hotel."

Maybe it is a fantastic value or maybe it's a cockroach infested dive.

Do not get emotionally involved with a prostitute

When men come to Thailand and hit the red-light area in the country, all of the sudden life changes. They become more handsome than they ever dreamed, compared to some Thais, they are wealthier than they thought, and they are good enough to land a good looking woman that back home they never had a chance to be with. Of course, in most cases all bets are off if there's no money involved.

Prostitutes work for money. They provide their body and sex in exchange for money. Prostitution is the world's oldest profession, yet when many foreigners come to Thailand, working girls somehow morph into love interests. Instead of having a couple of hours for fun, some foreigners forget everything and start believing the hype.

Learn to speak basic Thai before getting into a serious relationship

Romantics like the idea of falling in love without being able to speak the same language as their partner; realists know otherwise. Being unable to understand one another is like having a Ferrari but not knowing how to drive. Sure, you can learn to drive on your own, but you might crash and burn doing so. At the very least, learn to speak basic Thai before getting involved in a serious relationship.

Learn to speak, read, and write in proper Thai

This means go to a legitimate school. Sure, the neighbor can teach you, Nid or Noi from the local go-go bar can stop by at 2:00AM and teach you bar girl Thai, but learning the language from a good school or teacher can make a huge difference. Learn to speak proper, polite Thai. Doing so will set you apart from many other expats.

If your woman is working as a prostitute, do not expect her to be faithful

This would seem to be common sense and yet men all over the world have their hearts broken when they find out their big, big honey is sleeping with other men.

Resist the temptation to be Captain-Save-a-Ho

There is nothing wrong with being nice. There are men who come to Thailand and believe everything they are told and everything they hear. If the precious little honey you just met starts crying poor and asks for money, dump her. After all, wouldn't you prefer to have a woman capable of taking care of herself and free from any serious problems? There is no reason to be heartless, but know there is a fine line between giving a woman money because she is starving and giving them money to pay their bills.

If you are tempted to give a woman money or take care of her, ask yourself if she was okay before she met you and if she'll be okay if you're no longer around.

Never give more money than you can afford to lose

If you decide to forego the previous tenet, give no more than you can afford to lose. You are better off keeping your money for your own emergencies than giving it away. You never know what will happen; remember the 7 P's.

"Give a man a fish, and you feed him for a day; show him how to catch fish, and you feed him for a lifetime."

Instead of giving your girlfriend money that will never be returned, give her a job instead. Pay her to clean your house, act as your guide and translator, get something back for your money. This way you both benefit and your financial help is more than a one-off handout.

A polite and friendly Thai woman is much different from an interested Thai woman

You go into a restaurant, sit down and the waitress comes over to take your order. She is cute, very cute, so you flirt with her. In the course of your conversation she may ask where you are from, how long you will be in Thailand, and what you are doing here. She smiles, you smile, and the polite banter continues. Her English is cute, she's cute, so when you pay your bill, you decide to ask her out; nothing wrong with trying. You take the bill, set it down on the table, tenderly hold her hand and look into her eyes.

"Would you like to go somewhere with me?"

She smiles, turns away, slowly withdraws her hand, and walks back to the register with your money.

You thought there was chemistry. In fact, you thought she was into you. Obviously you were wrong. You get up to leave, she gives you her best *wai*, you both give half-hearted smiles, and you walk out wondering what just happened. Thai women are generally very friendly and polite and even if they find your unattractive they will do their best to be friendly.

She might actually like you but it may take time to get her to go out with you. The only way to get past this is to keep going to wherever she works, slowly getting to know her. Then you will learn if you are a customer or a romantic interest.

Thai Man No Good!

"Thai man no good!" is a sentence you may hear at some point in your time in Thailand. If Thai men are no good, why are so many Thai women married to them? Maybe the woman had a bad experience and was hurt by a Thai boyfriend or husband, maybe she's a huge pain in the ass, perhaps she has unrealistic expectations, or maybe she ran at the first sign of trouble. Maybe the man realized she wasn't someone he wanted to be with or she began whoring around when money got tight. The takeaway here is do not buy into the bullshit. Thai men are like any other men on the planet; there are good and bad and plenty who are sincere and committed to their loved ones.

Online Love Affairs are a Long Shot

She is in Thailand, you are not. Until you find a way to bridge this gap, the internet might as well be a million miles away. She might be a decent girl, she might even be a girl worth marrying, but Skyping and texting her daily just won't cut it. Until you meet her in person and get to know how she carries herself in daily life, you do not know her.

Even if you spend four hours a day online speaking with each other, you are taking her word as to what she is doing the remainder of the day. For all you know she talks to you while her husband is working. For all you know she has a boyfriend or is married and he works outside of Thailand.

Before professing your love for a woman, get to know her in person! Before committing yourself, spend time with her. Make several trips to Thailand, visit with her family and friends, and if possible, bring her to your country. The more time that passes the easier it will become to determine what is real and what is a charade.

Keep your expectations in check and do not let her pressure you into marriage or a long-term commitment because *this is how it's done in Thailand*. Make sure you both communicate your plans to one another before making promises to love one another till death do you part. Marriage is a gamble, but if you give the relationship time to grow, you'll get to know her past the initial politeness phase.

If the relationship lasts this far, then you need to figure out where you're going to live and how you're going to manage financially. If you're extremely lucky, the relationship might just work. I wouldn't count on it though.

A whore can present herself as a lady and a lady can present herself as a whore

A woman working in an office or bank can be every bit the whore as a bar girl. A woman who works outside of the service industry can rip you off or steal from you just as easily as one working in a bar.

Getting involved in drugs in Thailand is a losing proposition

They Call Me Farang

If you're visiting, wait to get home. If you're living in Thailand, you should know better. If you're an addict, get help. I have been inside two prisons covering boxing events; prisons are unpleasant, even as a visitor. Watch the movies Midnight Express and Return to Paradise before going to score that lid of herb or buying those tabs of ecstasy. Not to be a prude — when I was younger I used pot, mushrooms, cocaine, Qualuudes; everything except heroin and ecstasy, but Thailand has harsh penalties for drug users. It's not worth it.

Keep a low profile

Fly under the radar and avoid flaunting your wealth.

You are a man, act like one

Women in Asia expect you to be the man. Act like one. Figure it out.

Think with the big head, not the little one

Again, figure this one out. Use your brain and do not let your pecker make your decisions.

All Thai women are not for sale

Need I say more?

All Thai women might not be women. If you're unsure of your partner's gender, move on.

Unless you're into this sort of thing.

If you have a problem with a taxi driver, get out

Most problems with taxi drivers are avoidable. Make sure the driver knows where you want to go and the route you want to take prior to departing. One would think drivers would always have change for a hundred baht but the truth is, sometimes they do not. It is your responsibility to give them the correct amount, at least in their eyes.

Use metered taxis

There is no reason to use an unmetered taxi.

If you're on holiday, you should give yourself plenty of time to get where you want to go. Set up your life/trip to where if something goes wrong it's not a big deal.

If a driver refuses to turn on his meter, write down the taxi number and find another taxi. If he takes off and refuses to turn the meter on, immediately tell him you want to get out.

If you are staying at a hotel and there are drivers sitting outside waiting to take you somewhere, make sure they use the meter. Any decent hotel should make sure you have the option of taking a metered taxi. If they refuse, find another hotel.

Avoid Tuk-Tuks and Jet Skis

You're walking down the street and a Thai man with a big smile walks up to you.

"Hello, my friend! You want lady? Tuk-tuk?"

"No, no thank you," you reply.

"I give you good price. Fifty baht all day, we go to temple, I take you for lady."

If it's too good to be true, it probably is. Never let any driver take you to a massage parlor or hotel. You'll pay the original price plus his commission.

In the case of tuk-tuk drivers, most are out to make a quick buck and are nothing more than scoundrels. Nothing wrong with earning a living, however, when you want to go to Khao San Road and end up at a gem store, there's a problem.

If you must use a tuk-tuk (I avoid them like the plague),

get a Thai friend to help you with the negotiations, or better yet, to go with you.

When I first came to Thailand, I felt sorry for this poor fellow standing next to his tuk-tuk. He drove me to a temple where I was promptly told 'Today is very special day, no tax on gems. I have beautiful ruby for you.'

I knew it was a scam and declined.

Then he begged me to go to a gem store.

"They give me gas coupon."

I told him no and he went anyway. I screamed at him to stop and he refused. When traffic forced him to slow down at a stop light, I jumped out. Then came 30 minutes of him driving alongside of me, groveling for 100 baht. Eventually, I threw him the 100 baht and grabbed a taxi to Mah Boon Krong.

Don't even think about renting a jet ski. You might get away without getting stung, but many jet ski operators still attempt to extort money from foreigners. Again, it's not worth it.

Exit taxi's rear end first

I lost count of all the items I have lost in taxis. Three or four cellular phones, water bottles, and once, a backpack containing my marriage certificate and my son's birth certificates. Exit the taxi rear end first so you're looking into the taxi. Then if you leave something behind, there's a good chance you'll see it before the taxi takes off.

The End

Made in the USA
San Bernardino, CA
29 April 2018